D0119356

"We're all in this together - by ourselves"
Lily Tomlin

HIDDEN KITCHENS

OF

THE NORTH

With best wishes from Claire Macdonald of Macdonald

In aid of The Grampian Autistic Society

First Published in 1998 by Mrs Maureen E. Forbes-Gray, Waterton Mill, Waterton By Ellon, Aberdeenshire, Scotland, AB41 9QQ, on behalf of The Grampian Autistic Society.

ISBN 0-9533551-0-1
Designed by Maureen E. Forbes-Gray, Catherine Ferrier, Cathy Kyle and Mhairi McLean
Printed and bound in Scotland by Gilcomston Litho Limited

TO MUM

"A most loved Grandma, for her unconditional love for her grandchildren,

For that special hug meant only for her,

For that glance only she can give,

For the time she gives that only a Grandma can."

May I commend to you this wonderful cookery book. It has some immensely exciting recipes from all the best Hotels and Restaurants within an easy drive of the Grampian Region. I think you will find it quite fascinating.

Even more important I commend to you The Grampian Autistic Society. Autism is a very sad disorder and needs to be helped in every way. Autistic children are a great joy and they have a lot to offer but, we need to understand and to care for them. This cookery book will not only help the society financially, but will raise awareness to this most complex disorder.

Lady Aberdeen

INTRODUCTION

BY

JANE ASHER

Ever since I was a child I've enjoyed good food, and one of my favourite treats has always been to go out for a meal to a hotel or restaurant. Since having a family of my own, of course, eating out has become something we do less often, and I sometimes feel I'm missing out on some of the delicious menus that chefs all over the country are now producing.

Now here's the answer to that problem: this magnificent book is going to inspire me to create some wonderful restaurant meals at home. The standard of cuisine represented in these pages is extraordinary (I've always been a particular fan of Scottish cookery, in any case). There are dishes here to suit the smartest dinner party or coziest meal for two.

I have another very important reason for supporting this terrific book. For many years I have worked with adults and children with Autism. It is a devastating, perplexing condition that is still much misunderstood and of which many people - and indeed many health professionals - are not fully aware. One thing is certain: with help, and especially with early intervention - enormous gains can be made. The individual can be given the chance to develop to their fullest possible potential. New approaches and initiatives are being developed all the time, and it is vital that each of these is given a proper chance to be fully explored and evaluated. Children are still being diagnosed far too late; many of them fail to find the care in their area that their families so desperately want for them, and many adults with Autism are still not being found places where they can be helped to live fuller, happier lives.

A child with Autism, without proper care, can be effectively shut in a sad, terrifying and lonely world where everything outside is mysterious and incomprehensible. A large part of the happiness my husband and I derive from our three children is in the spontaneous and unthinking expressions of love that pass between us everyday: a quick kiss as they leave for a school, a cuddle when they're upset, or a whispered 'I love you mum and dad' at bedtime. It is easy to take these things for granted. With Autism the natural instinct you have to reach out and hug a frightened child may not be enough. It may well be rejected and misunderstood.

I have seen at first hand the difference that caring professional help can make to children with Autism and their families. Any project that raises money towards exploring new initiatives and helping more children to have a chance to realise their potential has my wholehearted support. I'm sure that you'll enjoy this delightful book as much as I, and on behalf of all those families affected by Autism, thank you for buying it and helping them to find a way forward.

Jane Asher
President, National Autistic Society.

MAUREEN'S INTRODUCTION

I feel very lucky to have found such purpose in the creation of the 'Hidden Kitchens of the North' which brings together the love for my child and my passion for cookery. Alexander is our seven-year-old son, who on the outside looks like any other boy. Even his loudness, energy and happy exuberance resembles other seven year olds, but underneath he is a child full of mystery and complexity.

It is possible that behind the barrier of this behaviour he is very bright. We have glimpses that give us hope. Like many Autistic children, Alex is a handsome chap. Unfortunately his social behaviour doesn't match up. It is very hard for parents, when these normal looking children appear to a bystander, as merely naughty and destructive. His inability to read human reaction and response will always limit his potential. It is very sad to have to teach a child to kiss you good night and we wonder if one day the ritual will join up with the emotion, and then the gesture will be complete.

However, Alex brings Chris, Anna and I so much joy and he earns the love of family, friends and neighbours. Life is never dull, and often full of fun, I never know what is round the next corner.

Alex was three years old when he was diagnosed as having Autism, he avoided eye contact with us and seemed not to understand instructions. The Grampian Autistic Society gave us practical advice and support when we needed it most. We are indebted to them for their help.

THE GRAMPIAN AUTISTIC SOCIETY

Ten years ago when there was very little help available, a handful of parents formed a support group. At this time Autism was barely recognised, and teachers and doctors were not equipped to help. Today the society raises awareness and campaigns for services and support. The newly refurbished Jigsaw Centre provides an invaluable source of support to families with Autistic children.

However in a climate of shrinking budgets it is imperative to create more funds. There is so much that can be done, and of course, our most important resource is people.

The staff are dedicated and experienced and, under less pressure could spend more time on research and evaluating treatment. We are trying so hard to make the pieces of the jigsaw fit together.

This is the third charity cook book I have worked on. So perhaps it's not surprising that apart from cookery demonstrations the practical applications of my Cordon Bleu training have taken a back seat.

Now with this book, what fun to be able to sneak into the kitchens of all these wonderful hotels and restaurants and persuade the chefs to part with their secrets. Each establishment was asked to contribute recipes for a starter, main course and dessert. Despite their busy schedules they managed to find time to generously share their recipes, all writing in their own inimitable style. Some are very logical and some read like a story.

We hope that we can tempt you to try some of the excellent recipes from famous eating establishments in the North of Scotland. If I can raise funds to shed light on this baffling disorder and raise public awareness I will have achieved my goal in creating this book. It has been an absolute pleasure for me to share my love of cooking with enthusiastic supporters in the catering industry. I know whatever I say can never convey enough my heartfelt thanks to all who have contributed.

ACKNOWLEDGEMENTS

To my family especially Mum and Auntie Maggie, both of whom my son, Alexander, adores. To my husband Chris and daughter Anna, for their encouragement and support. Life would be very hard without my family. I count myself lucky.

To Frank, Hilda and Dad, very much missed but who I know would have been right behind me every inch of the way.

To Mhairi McLean, a dear friend: this book would not have come to be without her unending support and hard work.

To Berry and Stuart for all their incredible photographic skills, time and patience which they have so willingly given to this project.

To Catherine who has a multitude of talents: being an artist is but only one string of her bow, I cannot thank her enough.

To Mary Kew and her friends in Aboyne for their valiant fund-raising efforts. Mary is chairperson of the Kieran Silcock Fund. Kieran is a two-year-old boy from Aboyne with Autism. Maria Silcock and Kieran are more new friends from this project.

To Chris Wooley, who somehow managed to completely proof read the whole book and look after her four children, one of whom is Autistic and in Alexander's class at school. Nigel her husband, did a fantastic job fund-raising for the book. A thank you will never be enough to both of them.

To Gill Howe and her group of proof readers, Gill is a very dear friend always willing to help, regardless of whatever life is throwing at her. Thank you to Sarah Meldrum, Hannah Vaughan, Cathy Kyle and Valerie Ramshaw.

To Jacky who kindly professionally proof read the final copy for us.

To James Mortimer, photographer, for the pictures of myself and Alexander and Christopher, Laurie, and mum Fiona.

To Rose, Brian, Lyn and Sam at the Jigsaw Centre, thank you for your patience, time and understanding.

To Steve Ritchie for his engraving of Collieston Pier.

To John and Sheila, who most generously gave money on behalf of the New Inn Outside Catering Staff, and to Lindsey and Catherine Halliday. My father would have been so pleased that all his staff/friends supported me in this project.

Thank you to the staff at Broadarrow, especially Peter Hall for helping us pull the book together in the final stages.

To David Barbour and Dorothy at Gilcomston Litho.

To all who have given very large and small sums of money: every penny is appreciated.

I hope I have not missed anyone out, I apologise now if I have done so.

Thank you one and all

Maureen

CONTENTS

Ardoe House Hotel
Starter

Ardoe House Hotel
Main Course

Ardoe House Hotel
Pudding

Cameron House Hotel
Starter

Cameron House Hotel
Main Course

Cameron House Hotel
Pudding

THE ARDOE HOUSE HOTEL

On the South Deeside road three miles west of Aberdeen, Ardoe House Hotel, a most elegant country house hotel, can be found standing in its own grounds. Ardoe House was built in 1837 by a wealthy soap manufacturer 'Soapie Ogston' for his wife. The character of the building is unrivalled in the area, using local granite as the building material, creating a baronial mansion with crow-stepped gables and cobbled bartizans. A most stunning building outside and in, where the large rooms lend themselves to conferences, weddings and private functions, surrounded by decor carefully chosen to enhance every detail of the original building.

It was very fortunate that I went to Ardoe House Hotel early on in the book project. The staff were so enthusiastic that it gave me the encouragement and confidence to 'go for it'! I am particularly grateful to Ewan Kirkpatrick, manager of Ardoe for his down-to-earth honest approach and suggestions which I really appreciated. Sous Chef Martin Ward has supported and encouraged me throughout my efforts with the cookery book. In addition to his expertise with food, Martin also has genuine interest and concern for the children involved. He has been extremely accommodating with his time, always managing to fit me into his extremely hectic schedule. His natural brilliance in the kitchen won him 'Young Chef of the Year 1997': the award-winning recipes we are fortunate to have for our book. The hotel has two AA rosettes.

Martin and I also decided he should create six of his favourite puddings to promote the launch of our book, which Ardoe is very kindly hosting for us. Sorry it will be all over by the time you read this, but I intend to savour every mouthful on your behalf!

Roasted Aubergine and Rabbit Soup with Essence of Truffle

Ingredients

1 sprig parsley	2 potatoes (peeled)
3 aubergines	3 teaspoons of truffle oil
1 rabbit	¼ pt of port wine
1 bulb fennel (roughly chopped)	1 pt vegetable oil (confit rabbit legs) *
1 onion (roughly chopped)	30g of thyme
2 garlic cloves (roughly chopped)	2 pts of chicken stock
2 small carrots (roughly chopped)	1 tomato
1 leek (roughly chopped)	¼ pint of cream
1 tablespoon of tomato puree Seasoning	
* see glossary	

Method

Remove the fillets and legs from the rabbit. Trim up the rabbit legs and place into the oil with the garlic, onion, seasoning and thyme. Cook for 1 hour on 200°C/400°F/gas mark 6.

In an oven tray roast off the remaining rabbit carcass and fillets, once brown add the rest of the vegetables. Cook out for 10 minutes.

Add the tomato puree and port, let it reduce down to a glaze and then add the chicken stock. Cook for a further 30 minutes. Remove the rabbit carcass and throw away. Take the rest of the soup and place it into the food processor, blend for 5 minutes. Remove the soup from the blender and pass through a fine sieve. Finish with cream and truffle oil.

For the rabbit leg, remove from oil once cool and dice the leg meat. Place in a bowl adding the finished soup.

Garnish with parsley and tomato concassée (to concassée the tomato, remove skin and seeds, finely chop). (Serves 4)

Ballotine of Salmon & Scallop served with a Risotto of Chives, Roasted Parsnips, Baby Fondant Potatoes and Pine Kernel Sauce

Ingredients

2 scallops
1½lbs salmon and skin
4oz spinach
2 jacket potatoes
2 parsnips
8oz of butter
1oz of pine kernels
4oz Risotto rice
1oz of pancetta
1 tablespoon of honey

2 pints of chicken stock
2oz of chives
1 tablespoon truffle oil
1 clove garlic
1 shallot
¾ pint of cream
Salt and pepper
3 baby carrots (cooked)
1 chicken stock cube

Method

For the Salmon
Take the two scallops and remove the roe. Place one thin slice of pancetta around the scallops. In boiling water blanch the spinach for 30 seconds and then remove into iced water. Take some of the blanched spinach and wrap it around the pancetta.

Take the salmon and remove the scales and the skin. Cut the salmon into 2cm thick strips (lengthways). Wrap this around the scallops you prepared earlier so that you end up with a spiral shape. Do the same process with the salmon skins. Seal both sides of the salmon and cook for 8 minutes on 200°C/400°F/gas mark 6.

For the Risotto
Bring one pint of the chicken stock to the boil, add the risotto rice and cook to the bite, about 20 minutes. Take off the heat and fold in 2oz of butter, ¼ pint of cream and chopped chives. Season to taste.

For the Fondant
Take a flat-based pan and line it with thin slices of the remaining butter. Cut potatoes into squares of about 7cm wide and 4cm deep. Place these flat down onto the butter.

Add the remaining chicken stock to the pan. Place on heat and cook until the liquid has reduced and the butter has been absorbed into the potatoes.

For the Parsnips
Top and tail the parsnips, peel the outside skin off and place onto an oven tray with butter and a spoonful of honey. Season and then place in the oven until golden brown.

For the Sauce
Bring ½ pint of cream to the boil with the chicken stock cube crushed into it. In another pan roast off the pine kernels and 1 clove of garlic with the finely diced shallot, then add in the remaining spinach. Mix cream and spinach mixture together, place in a food processor and blend until smooth. Add truffle oil and mix well.

For the Presentation
Take the risotto and place onto the plate in a circular shape. Place the cooked salmon on top. Take the roasted parsnips and stand upright to the right of the salmon. Place the fondant potato in between the salmon and the parsnips. Place the three carrots on the top of the parsnips and then drizzle the sauce around the salmon and serve. (Serves 4)

A Rich Chocolate and Whisky Mousse served with Crisp Praline, Clotted Cream and Orange Syrup

Ingredients

100g caster sugar
200g salted butter
1 tablespoon of glucose liquid
25g icing sugar
2 tablespoons of clotted cream

300g dark chocolate
3 eggs
1 double measure of whisky
25g cocoa powder

Praline
75g caster sugar
25g almonds roasted
25g glucose liquid

25g hazelnuts roasted
3 drops of lemon juice

Tuille Paste
175g flour
125g melted butter
25g icing sugar

175g caster sugar
3 ½ egg whites

Orange Syrup
75g caster sugar
¼ pint of water

Zest of 1 orange
¼ pint of orange juice

Method

For the Mousse
Melt butter and chocolate separately over a Bain-marie. Whisk egg whites and sugar to ribbon stage. Add the chocolate, glucose and butter together then fold into the eggs and sugar.

Place the mixture into moulds and cook for 6 minutes on 180°C/350°F/gas mark 4, remove from oven and chill. Once cool remove from the mould and take a thin slice off the bottom of the mousse. Take a steel skewer and place a hole into the mousse making sure that the hole does not go all the way through. Take the whisky and pour into the hole, seal the hole up with the bottom of the mousse that you cut off earlier.

For the Praline
Place the water, sugar, glucose and lemon juice into a thick-bottomed pan. Bring to the boil with as little stirring as possible until golden brown. Add the nuts, and then pour onto a marble slab.

Roll praline out until about 2cm thick. Cut out a triangle shape with a sharp knife.

For the Tuille Paste
Melt the butter in a microwave or over a Bain-marie. Place the flour and sugar into a mixing bowl. Add this to the egg whites, followed by the melted butter, mixing together until you have a smooth paste. Place the mixture into the fridge and allow to cool.

To make the Biscuit
Take the Tuille paste and spread it onto greaseproof paper in the shape of a pencil. Place into the oven at 220°C /400°F/ gas mark 6 for 2-3 minutes or until golden brown. Take out of the oven and allow to cool. Sprinkle with icing sugar.

For the Orange Syrup
Zest one orange. Take the zest and place into boiling water for 30 seconds then refresh into cold water (do this 7 times). Place the sugar and water into a pan. Bring to the boil and then add in the orange juice and zest. Reduce the liquid to a thick syrup.

For the Presentation
Place the mousse at the left hand side of the plate. Place the triangle of praline at the back of the mousse so that it stands upright against the mousse. With two spoons shape the clotted cream and place to the bottom right of the mousse. Place your Tuille pencil biscuit into the clotted cream and rest the end onto the praline triangle. Take the orange syrup and place around the edge of the plate, dust with cocoa powder and serve.
(Serves 4)

Summer Pudding

Ingredients

8oz strawberries	*8oz blackcurrants*
8oz raspberries	*2 tablsp of creme de cassis*
8oz blackberries	*1pt water*
12oz caster sugar	*16 slices of white bread*

Method

For this recipe you will need 8 x 150ml moulds.

Bring the water and sugar to the boil. Add to this all of the fruits and simmer for about 10 minutes or until the fruits are soft but still whole. Remove from the heat and drain off the liquid into a clean pan. Place back onto the heat and reduce by half so that you have a semi-thick sauce.

Take the bread and remove crusts. Dip each slice of bread into the sauce and line all the moulds remembering to overlap the bread. Now take the soft fruits and fill the moulds, finish by covering with more bread. Place the moulds into the fridge with a weight on top of them to help press the summer pudding. Chill for about 3 hours.

Save any remaining fruits and sauce as this could come in handy for a garnish for the dessert.

Turn out the summer pudding onto a plate. Cover with the remaining sauce and place a little of the fruits to the side of the pudding. You are now ready to indulge. (Serves 8)

"Happy Eating"

Crème Caramel

Ingredients

For the Caramel :
10oz caster sugar
100ml water

For the Crème :
4 eggs   *½ litre milk*
4 egg yolks   *1 vanilla pod cut in half*
9oz caster sugar   *½ litre double cream*

Method

For this recipe you will need 8 (3 x 3cm) Dariole moulds.

Bring the sugar and water to the boil and reduce until the solution turns into a light golden-brown caramel. Remove from the heat and divide the caramel into the Dariole moulds. There should be enough caramel to line all the moulds.

For the crème, pre-heat the oven to 140°C/275°F/gas mark 1. Mix the whole eggs, egg yolks and sugar together, add in the cream, milk and vanilla pod and whisk. Pass the mixture through a strainer into a clean basin.

Pour the mixture into the Dariole moulds. Place the moulds into a tray of warm water which should come half way up the Dariole moulds. Place into the pre-heated oven and cook for 40-50 minutes. Remove from oven and allow to cool.

To serve turn out of the mould onto a plate so that the caramel surrounds the crème caramel. (Serves 8)

Sticky Toffee Pudding with Butterscotch Sauce

Ingredients
3 tablsp coffee powder.
10oz dates (stoned)
500ml water
2 teaspoons bicarbonate of soda
4oz butter
10oz sugar (demerara)

3 egg yolks
4 eggs (beaten)
10oz self-raising flour
2 teaspoons rum essence
2 teaspoons nutmeg

For the Sauce :
300ml double cream
300ml single cream
4 teaspoons treacle

4oz demerara sugar
1 tsp ginger

Method

Pre-heat oven to 170°C/325°F/gas mark 3. Grease a 12in x 12in baking tray.

Take the dates, coffee and water, place into a pan and bring to the boil. Once the dates are soft, place the dates, water and coffee into a food processor and blend. Remove from the blender and place into a large mixing bowl. Fold in the bicarbonate of soda.

Cream the butter and sugar together until fluffy, add the eggs and beat well. Mix in the dates, flour, nutmeg and rum essence. Pour the mixture into the greased baking tray and cook a pre-heated oven for about 40-50 minutes or until firm to touch, without browning.

To make the sauce simply, place all the ingredients into a pan and bring to the boil, stirring continuously. (Serves 8)

Enjoy your pudding never mind the calories!

Bread and Butter Pudding

Ingredients

10 slices of white bread
10oz soft butter (for spreading on bread)
400ml double cream
200ml milk
2oz sultanas

2oz currants
2oz raisins
1 fresh vanilla pod
6oz caster sugar
6 egg yolks
2 tsp. grated nutmeg

Method

Pre-heat oven to 170°C/325°F/gas mark 3. Grease a 3 pint pudding basin.

Butter each slice of bread and then remove the crusts with a sharp knife. Place the milk and cream together into a pan. Split the vanilla pod and add this to the milk and cream. Bring the milk and cream mixture to the boil. Whisk the egg yolks and caster sugar in a bowl until they reach a soft peak, add in the nutmeg, boiling cream and milk and whisk. Arrange the bread in layers, sprinkling each layer with sultanas, currants and raisins, finish off with a layer of bread. The warm egg mixture may now be poured over the bread. Let the bread and butter pudding rest for 20 minutes. Place the dish into a roasting tray and fill three quarters full of warm water. Place into the pre-heated oven and cook for 20 minutes.

Remove from the oven, sprinkle with icing sugar and serve. (Serves 4-6)

Dessert

Glazed Lemon Tart

Ingredients

For the Sweet Pastry :
400g plain flour
100g caster sugar
1 vanilla pod
200g unsalted butter
1 egg
2 tablsp water

For the Lemon Tart Mix :
6 eggs
7 lemons zest & juice
½ litre double cream
175g caster sugar

Method

For the sweet pastry sieve the flour and sugar into a bowl. Split the vanilla pod and scrape the seeds into the flour. Rub in the butter to give a bread crumb texture. Beat the egg and water together and work this into the mix to form a dough. Wrap the mixture in clingfilm and leave to rest for 30 minutes.

Pre-heat oven to 180°C/350°F/gas mark 4.

Roll out the pastry to ¼" thick and line a 10" flan tin. Line the pastry with grease proof paper and fill with baking beans. Bake blind in the pre-heated oven for 10-15 minutes, or until the pastry is a light golden brown. Remove the grease-proof paper and baking beans and leave to cool. Reduce oven temperature to 140°C/275°F/gas mark 1.

For the lemon tart mixture, mix the eggs and sugar in a bowl until smooth, but don't beat. Pour in the cream and mix in the lemon juice and zest. Pour the mixture into the pre-baked flan case and bake in the pre-heated oven for 45 minutes until the tart has just set.

Remove from the oven and allow to cool. The lemon tart is now ready to be served. (Serves 8-12)

Dessert

Deep Fried Strawberries with Mango Coulis and Chantilly Cream

Ingredients

For the Fritters :
24 strawberries
200ml apple juice
3oz plain flour
2oz sugar
1 sprig of fresh mint (garnish)
1 pint vegetable oil (deep frying strawberries)
100ml strawberry liqueur
1oz self raising flour

For the Coulis :
6oz caster sugar
200ml water
12oz fresh mango
1 vanilla pod
1 tablsp liquid glucose

For the Chantilly Cream :
¼pt whipping cream
2oz soft brown sugar
Pinch nutmeg

Method

Pre-heat pan of vegetable oil. To make the mango coulis, bring to the boil the sugar and water, split the vanilla pod and add it to the sugar and water. Add the mango and cook until it is soft. Place into a food processor and purée. Remove from the food processor, pass through a sieve into a clean pan and add the liquid glucose. Place back onto the heat and reduce by half or until you have a thick syrup.

To make the batter, mix the apple juice, strawberry liqueur, flours and sugar together. Remove the stalks from the strawberries and lightly flour each piece. Dip each strawberry into the batter mix and deep fry in hot oil until they are golden-brown and crispy. Drain well and sprinkle with sugar. To make the Chantilly cream, whip the cream until it is holding its shape. Fold in the caster sugar and nutmeg. Serve. (Serves 4-6)

Marion Macfarlane is a shining example of the excellent standard of cooking that flourishes in the North-East of Scotland. From her background as a teacher, with a true love of good Scottish produce, she went on to win Masterchef 1995.

I felt she must have a place in our book as a true representative of all that's good in Scottish cooking. Just wait till you taste the Tangy Lemon and Bramble Tart, Yum!

Scallop and Crab Mousseline with a Champagne Butter

Ingredients

210g (7 ½oz) prepared scallops with corals
1 teaspoon salt
Freshly ground white pepper
1 medium egg
150ml (5fl oz) double cream
55ml (2fl oz) soured cream
50g-75g (2-3oz) white crabmeat
4 whole king scallops (without corals)

For the Sauce :
110ml (4fl oz) fish stock
150ml (5fl oz) champagne
160g (5 ½oz) unsalted butter (chilled and cut into cubes)
2 tablespoons double cream
1 tablespoon finely chopped chives
Fennel, chervil or dill to garnish

Method

Process the 210g (7 ½oz) of scallops with the salt and pepper till smooth, first removing the membrane surrounding the flesh. Add the egg and process for one minute. Remove and chill until required (at least 30 minutes). Gradually fold in both the cream and the soured cream.

Butter 4 Dariole moulds or ramekins and half fill with the mixture. Add a layer of white crab meat. Now top with the rest of the scallop mousseline. Settle the mixture by bumping gently on worksurface. Cover each with greaseproof paper. Put a folded newspaper in a roasting pan and place the moulds on top. Add enough water to come to half way up the mould. Bake at 180°C/350°F/gas mark 4 for 25 minutes. Leave to sit for a few minutes before demoulding onto a warmed plate.

For the champagne butter sauce, place the fish stock and champagne in a small pot and cook over a high heat until reduced by half. Turn the heat down and whisk in the butter little by little then season and add the cream.

Taste, and add a final splash of champagne if needed. Set aside and keep warm while you plate up the mousses. Add chives to the sauce just before serving.

To make the rosettes, cut out and butter four 3-inch squares of foil. Cut the 4 remaining scallops into 5 thin slices and arrange in an overlapping circle on a piece of the foil. Brush the top of each with melted butter. Place them in a steamer, cover and steam for about 1½ minutes. Carefully position on top of each cooked mousseline and garnish with sprigs of the fresh herbs suggested. (Serves 4)

Chef's Tip

The coral is part of the scallop, often referred to as the roe. The bright pinkish colour of the coral is easily distinguished from the rest of the scallop which is white. Remember to remove the thick white muscle around the outside of the scallop before using.

Roasted Quails with Wild Mushrooms in a Madeira Sauce

Ingredients

6 quails
50g (2oz) unsalted butter (softened)
1 dessertspoon finely chopped parsley
1 small clove garlic (crushed)
1-2 teaspoons lemon juice
¼ teaspoon salt
1 dessertspoon of olive oil
220g (8fl oz) brown chicken stock
110ml (4fl oz) Madeira
Knob of unsalted butter
275g (12oz) mixed wild mushrooms (chopped)
25g (1oz) butter

Method

Starting at the neck end of each quail, loosen the skin and work your finger under the skin (it helps if you first oil your fingers slightly, also long nails cause problems!). You should be able to reach down the full length of the breast.

Place the butter, parsley, garlic, lemon juice and salt in a small bowl and beat until smooth. Carefully push about a teaspoonful of this mixture down each side of the breast under the skin and smooth out with your fingers. Place covered in the fridge for at least 6 hours or overnight. Remove from the fridge half an hour before cooking.

Heat 1 dessertspoon of oil in a roasting pan and quickly sear the quails on all sides. Place each quail on its side and roast in a pre-heated oven at 230°C /450°F/gas mark 8 for 5 minutes. Turn each quail on to its other side and roast for 5 minutes. Now turn them onto their backs and cook for a further 6-7 minutes.

Remove the quails from the tin, tipping out the juices from inside each quail into the container with your stock. Leave the quails to rest in a warm place while you finish the sauce.

Remove the excess fat from the roasting tin and, over a high heat, deglaze with the Madeira. Add the stock and boil vigorously to reduce to about half its original volume. Strain the sauce, if necessary, reheat and whisk in a knob of unsalted butter and season, if required.

To cook the mushrooms, heat a large frying pan until it's hot, add the butter and fry the mushrooms for 3-4 minutes until cooked. Season and add the parsley.

To serve, use strong kitchen scissors or better still, game scissors and cut each quail in half. I choose to arrange three halves around a tower of dauphinoise potatoes topped with hot grated beetroot and garnish with the wild mushrooms and the Madeira sauce. However many other seasonal vegetables could accompany this dish. (Serves 4)

Tangy Lemon and Bramble Tart

Ingredients

For the pastry :
150g (5oz) plain flour
25g (1oz) icing sugar
110g (4oz) unsalted butter
Rind of 1 lemon
⅛ teaspoon natural vanilla essence

For the filling :
4 medium eggs
150g (5oz) caster sugar
Finely grated zest and juice of 3 lemons
150ml (¼pint) double cream
175g (6oz) bramble berries
Icing sugar to dust

Method

Preheat the oven to 190°C/375°F/gas mark 5.

To make the pastry, place the flour, icing sugar, butter, lemon rind and vanilla into a food processor and whizz until the mixture comes together to form a soft dough. Remove and knead lightly, then wrap in foil and refrigerate for at least one hour. Roll out the dough between two pieces of cling film to line a 23cm (9-inch) loose-bottomed flan-ring. Use the bottom sheet of cling film to lift the pastry and help smooth into the tin before removing. Prick the pastry and refrigerate for at least another hour (this will allow the pastry to relax again and will prevent shrinkage during cooking). Line the case with foil or paper and cook for 10 minutes. Remove from the oven and cool slightly while you make the filling. Turn down the oven to 170°C/325°F/gas mark 3.

Beat together the eggs and sugar until well blended but not frothy. Beat in the lemon juice and zest and then the double cream. Arrange the brambles in a single layer on the cooked base and pour on the lemon custard. Bake for 25-30 minutes until just set in the centre. Allow to cool and dust with icing sugar. Serve with vanilla ice cream, whipped cream, sweetened Mascarpone cheese or try the following Crème de Mure cream. (Serves 4-6)

Crème de Mure Cream

Ingredients

150ml (5fl oz) double cream
Caster sugar to taste
1 tablespoon Crème de Mure

Method

Lightly whip the double cream with a little caster sugar and fold in the liqueur. (Serves 4-6)

The Gleneagles Hotel
Starter

The Gleneagles Hotel
Main Course

The Gleneagles Hotel
Pudding

Faraday's
Starter

Faraday's
Main Course

Faraday's
Pudding

Cameron House Hotel sits on the banks of Loch Lomond, steeped in history and romance. Berry, Stuart and I were shown into the Georgian dining room overlooking the grounds and loch, where we spent the next few hours photographing the exquisite recipes they gave us for the book, amidst the laughter from the wedding taking place outside.

You must try the Double Baked Finnan Haddock Soufflé with Anchovy Butter. It does stand up well, and we should know, considering how long it took to photograph it! And it tastes "real fine to me". The dessert may look hard to reproduce but when you taste it, believe me, all is worthwhile.

This is the kind of place you want to go for a special occasion, even if you can only go one day!

Double-Baked Finnan Haddock Soufflé with Anchovy Butter

Ingredients

For the Sauce :

3 eggs
2oz flour
2oz butter
5oz Finnan haddock
13fl oz milk
2 anchovy fillets
4 well-buttered ramekins

2 shallots
½pt fish stock
¼pt cream
¼pt white wine
½oz butter
Chopped chives

Method

1   Cook the Finnan haddock in the milk. Strain milk off.

2   Add butter to flour to make roux.

3.   Add the milk to the roux.

4.   Allow to cool, when cool add egg yolks only, and mix well.

5.   Whisk egg whites until slightly stiff.

6.   Add the flaked Finnan haddock to the roux and fold in egg whites.

7.   Pour mix into well-buttered ramekins.

8.   Place ramekins in a Bain-marie and bake at 180°C/350°F/gas mark 4 for 30 minutes. When cooked turn out onto serving dish.

9.   Meanwhile finely chop the shallots and sauté in butter for 5-6 minutes, until they are soft and opaque.

10.   Add the white wine and reduce the quantity by half.

11.   Add the fish stock, cream and chopped chives.

12.   Finally, chop the anchovies, warm the fish sauce and arrange, together with warm soufflé, on the serving dish. (Serves 4)

Pan Fried Collops of Venison with Red Cabbage and a Redcurrant Sauce

Ingredients

12oz medallions of venison
½ red cabbage
½pt venison jus/stock
2 tablsp redcurrant jelly
1 glass red wine
1 sprig thyme
2 tablsp olive oil
1oz butter

2 ripe pears
1lb potatoes
Seasoning
1pt apple juice
2 tablsp brown sugar
2 tablsp cider vinegar
12 heads of asparagus
(placed in boiling water for 10 seconds)

Method

1. Thinly cut and slice the red cabbage. Cook in the apple juice, brown sugar and vinegar until the liquid has evaporated, then season.

2. Cook and puree the potatoes. Keep hot.

3. Seal the venison in a hot pan with olive oil, cook until nicely brown on the outside and still pink in the middle.

4. Remove the venison from the pan and deglaze the pan with the wine. Then add jus and thyme. Reduce to half quantity.

5. Cut the pears into small pearls or cubes and sauté in ½oz butter.

6. Melt the redcurrant jelly in saucepan and whisk in the rest of the butter. Serve in a sauceboat to accompany the main course.

7. Use a 4" round pastry cutter to centre the cabbage in the middle of the plate. Place the venison and collops around the cabbage. Use dessert spoons to make quenelles with the potatoes and place in between the collops. Pour round a little sauce. Scatter the pears round the edge. Arrange asparagus heads on top of venison collops (see picture). Serve immediately. (Serves 4)

Dessert

Oat Nougatine Layers Filled with a Honey and Malt Whisky Cream and Fresh Raspberries

Ingredients

For the Nougatine :
50g glucose liquid
100g fondant*
70g ground almonds
70g pinhead oatmeal
10g butter

For the Cream :
40g clear honey
20ml double cream
4ml whisky

For the Sauce :
1 punnet raspberries
5 leaves of mint
20ml water
50g sugar
½ lemon (juice only)
1 punnet raspberries (to fill layers)
Blueberries and blackberries for decoration
* see glossary

Method

Nougatine

1. Place glucose and fondant into a pan. Cook into a nice golden caramel.

2. Add butter, oatmeal and almonds, stir with a wooden spoon.

3. Process to a fine crumb in a food processor.

4. Spread the crumbs on to an oven tray covered with silicone paper. Gently heat through in the oven at 160°C/312°F/gas mark 2.

5. The crumbs will become firm, use a rolling pin to get an even surface, (work quickly otherwise the mixture becomes hard). Then use a 65mm plain scone cutter to punch out discs of nougatine, 3 discs per portion.

Cream

1. Whip the cream, add the honey and whisky (as chantilly cream).

Sauce

1. Boil the raspberries, mint, water and sugar in a pan until soft. Liquidise and pass through a sieve, then add the lemon juice.

To Assemble

1. Layer the nougatine discs in three layers, sandwiched by cream and raspberries making a tower effect. The final topping should be nougatine.

2. Pour round a little sauce, with blueberries and blackberries to decorate the plate.

3. Use a template or siliconised paper to create stripes on the top layer of nougatine with icing sugar. (Serves 4)

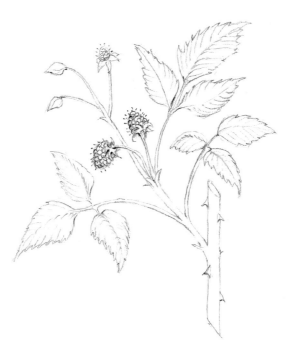

CASA SALVATORE

This is our local Italian Restaurant, and we love it! The Italians know how to eat, drink and have a good time, and I am all for that. Mr Salvatore is also famous, in the North-East of Scotland, for his operatic singing. This is a regular feature, as you enjoy the delights from the menu.

The restaurant is family run as you would expect: his wife and son play an important part, in ensuring the standard of cuisine is very high. People travel to eat here, and booking well in advance is recommended.

Instead of a pudding recipe, Mr Salvatore has kindly provided an alternative main course in the form of his most sought-after dish, Tagliatelle Salvatore. This can be very easily tried at home.

Buon Appetito!

P.S If you have never liked Chicken Livers, try these: you will be an immediate convert! - I certainly am.

Starter

Crostino Di Fegatini

Chicken Livers with Onions, Garlic, Wine and Cream over Hot Crusty Bread

Ingredients

2 tablespoons olive oil
1 medium onion, finely chopped
300g (11oz) chicken livers
1 clove garlic
2 large sprigs of fresh parsley
½ glass dry white wine
½ pint of chicken stock
¼ pint single cream
Freshly ground black pepper and salt
12 thin slices of crusty bread (baguette) 100cm (4 inches) in diameter

Method

First, wash and trim the chicken livers. Fry the garlic and onion gently in the oil for 5 minutes until soft, but not coloured. Add the livers and parsley, cook gently, stirring from time to time, for approximately 10-15 minutes until the livers are cooked.

Add the wine, allow the alcohol to evaporate for 2-3 minutes. Add chicken stock and cream, seasoning with salt and ground pepper, let it simmer for 5-10 minutes.

Grill the bread, place it onto a plate, spoon the chicken livers over, garnish with flat lettuce leaves, cucumber, wedges of tomato, a few slices of red onions and, to finish, sprinkle with parsley. (Serves 4)

Main Course

Tagliatelle Salvatore

Ingredients

4 tablespoons olive oil
1oz butter
2 medium-sized onions (diced)
500g tin plum tomatoes
250g mushrooms
250g red and green peppers
Salt and freshly ground black pepper
500g egg yellow tagliatelle
100g grated parmesan cheese
½ pint single cream

Method

Heat the oil in a large frying pan, add onions, strips of red and green peppers, sliced mushrooms and butter. Sauté gently over a low heat until tender and slightly coloured. Stir the mixture occasionally and add the diced plum tomatoes with their own juices.

Stirring well, add the cream and 50g of the parmesan, season this with salt and pepper. Cook over a gentle heat, until the mixture is quite thick. Meanwhile add the tagliatelle to a large pan of boiling water, adding a dessert spoon of salt and a spoon full of oil to prevent the pasta becoming sticky. Boil rapidly until the tagliatelle is tender but still firm ('Al dente' or firm to the bite).

Immediately drain the tagliatelle well. Mix tagliatelle with the sauce. Serve into a pasta bowl, sprinkling the dish with the rest of the parmesan cheese. (Serves 4)

Pollo Al Marsala

Chicken Breasts in Marsala Wine

Ingredients

4 tablespoons of olive oil
2oz butter
4 chicken breasts
2 medium size onions, skinned and finely chopped
250g sliced mushrooms
¼ pint of marsala wine or sweet sherry
¼ pint of chicken stock
½ pint single cream
1 bunch of fresh parsley
Seasoning

Method

Put the chicken breasts in a large frying pan with oil on a low heat, turning occasionally until they are golden brown all over. Remove chicken from the pan and keep warm by covering with tin foil. Add to the pan the butter, onions and mushrooms, stir well. Cook gently over a low heat for 5 minutes, stirring occasionally.

Return the chicken breasts to the frying pan, add marsala wine, chicken stock and cream, stirring well and turning the chicken breasts occasionally. Simmer gently for about 15 minutes until chicken is tender and cooked right through, and the sauce is reduced. Season with salt and pepper. Serve the chicken breasts with the sauce over the top, and sprinkle parsley over for decoration. (Serves 4)

THE COCK AND BULL

We were excited when The Cock and Bull opened just a few miles from our house. It is so good to encounter their wonderful fresh approach to food, making maximum use of Scottish produce, most especially our wonderful Scottish beef, game and seafood.

This restaurant used to be a quiet roadside Inn until the new owners transformed it into a busy eating establishment worth travelling for. The varied decor consists of a fascinating mix of collectibles. Well worth a visit!

Starter

Terrine of Goats Cheese Mousse with Mediterranean Vegetables and Pesto Dressing

Ingredients

For the Terrine :
500g goats cheese (fresh)
250g soft butter
½ pint double cream

For the Vegetables :
2 x red peppers
2 x yellow peppers
1 x aubergine
3 x tomatoes
3 x courgettes
½ lb large spinach leaves
½ pint olive oil
1 bunch thyme

For the Pesto :
50g pine kernels
50g garlic cloves
50g grated parmesan
30 basil leaves
200ml olive oil

Method

Prepare the vegetables; peel the peppers, tomatoes, courgettes, and the aubergine. Blanch the spinach then wrap the terrine mould with clingfilm and spinach. Cook all the vegetables in oil and season with salt and pepper. Chop the thyme and sprinkle over.

To make the mousse first mix the cheese to a smooth paste in a robot coupe, then add the soft butter and mix for one minute. Whip the cream and gently mix with the cheese. Season to taste. Build the terrine with the vegetables and the cheese. Leave in the fridge for 2 hours.

For the pesto, put all the ingredients in a blender and mix till a smooth paste is formed. To serve, cut a slice from the terrine when chilled, place on plate with pesto.

Pan Fried Salmon with Creamed Puy lentils and Langoustines

Ingredients

4 x escalopes of salmon (boned, with skin left on)
16 x pieces of langoustine
80g puy lentils
¼ pint chicken stock
¼ onion (roughly cut)
¼ carrot (roughly cut)
¼ leek (roughly cut)
½ bayleaf
½ sprig thyme
Cream
Brunoise (small and diced carrot, onion and leek)

Method

Wash lentils, add chicken stock, the roughly cut carrots, onions, the bayleaf and thyme. Bring to the boil, skim and simmer till almost cooked. When ready, drain lentils, retain stock and reduce. Add the Brunoise of small diced vegetables (carrot, onion, leek) and just cover with cream and keep warm.

Season Salmon skin only with sea salt. Pan fry skin-side down in olive oil till ¾ cooked and top is still pink, remove and keep warm. In the same pan, fry langoustine tails.

To serve: on a warm plate, spread out the hot seasoned lentils, place salmon, skin-side up, on top with the fried langoustine. (Serves 4)

Hot Chocolate Soufflé with Candied Kumquats

Ingredients

For the Soufflé :
160g bitter dark chocolate
6 egg whites
3 egg yolks
40g sugar
25g butter

For the Candied Kumquats :
12 kumquats.
100g icing sugar

Method

Pour 4 fl oz of boiling water over the kumquats. Remove the kumquats, add the icing sugar and reduce to a syrup.

Melt the chocolate. Whisk the egg white, add the sugar then the yolks. Combine with the chocolate. Pour into moulds or ramekins which have been lightly buttered and sugared. Cook in Bain-marie for 20 minutes at 190°C/375°F/gas mark 5. Serve hot with kumquats, a vanilla sauce, or cream. (Serves 4)

When we returned to Aberdeen after many years absence, The Courtyard was definitely 'the'; place to go - it still is! The restaurant is always packed out and you have to book well in advance. The Courtyard is to be found in a small cobbled lane, in Aberdeen's commercial district, so convenient for Aberdonians. If you wish for more informal surroundings, or have less time to linger, then Martha's Bistro downstairs serves the same menu.

The restaurant is run by owners Mr & Mrs Findlay, whose Head Chef Glen Lawson and his team, are well known for their innovative use of fish, game and poultry. The restaurant won the MacAllan Taste of Scotland Award in 1994.

Seared Tuna and Potato with a Vegetable Salsa

Ingredients

340g tuna loin
2 large potatoes
50g red peppers
50g yellow peppers
50g red onion
1 clove garlic
2 tomatoes
2 tablsp coriander
¼pt olive oil
1 lemon
1 red chilli
Seasoning

Method

1. Slice the tuna loin into 12 equal portions. Place in a single layer on a tray and brush with half of the lemon juice. Season well with cracked black pepper and rock salt. Place in fridge for 1 hour.

2. For the salsa, dice red and yellow peppers, chilli, garlic and red onion, mix together well. Add chopped coriander and juice from the other half of the lemon, season well. Add half the olive oil and mix well. Refrigerate until used.

3. Wash and scrub potatoes, leaving the skin on. Par boil in salted water for 5 minutes until you can insert the point of a sharp knife but it should not go all the way through.

4. Refresh potatoes in cold water, then cut into 12 slices of equal thickness.

5. Brush both sides of the potato with olive oil, using a very hot griddle pan, cook the potatoes through.

6. Repeat step 5 with the tuna.

7. Layer the potato and tuna on a serving plate and spoon the vegetable salsa around the top. (Serves 4)

Chef's Tip : Top this with a teaspoon of Greek yoghurt.

Saddle of Lamb wrapped in Spinach and Bacon with a Cherry Tomato Compote

Ingredients

1 short saddle of lamb (bones reserved for jus)
½ onion peeled and cut into chunks
2 sticks celery peeled and cut into chunks
½ leek peeled and cut into chunks
1 carrot peeled and cut into chunks
4 shallots peeled and cut into chunks
1 punnet cherry tomatoes
Thyme (a few sprigs)
4 basil leaves
Rosemary (a few sprigs)
Smoked back bacon 4-6 rashers
1lb fresh spinach
2 measures port
1 tablsp redcurrant jelly
White wine
2 tablsp tomato puree
Butter
½ clove garlic

Method

1. Stretch the back bacon on a chopping board using the back of a chopping knife. It should be the same size as the saddle of lamb.

2. Wash the spinach, carefully remove stalks, and blanch in boiling water for 2 minutes. Rinse in cold water to reserve the colour. Press the spinach between two plates to get rid of excess water. Lay on top of the bacon.

3. Roll lamb tightly in the bacon and spinach, secure with 3-4 cocktail sticks.

4. Brown the lamb in butter over a very high heat to seal all round. Place in an oven at 180°C/350°F/gas mark 4 for 15-18 minutes. The lamb should still be pink in the middle.

5. To make the sauce brown the lamb bones and onion, celery, leek and carrot at 200°C/400°F/gas mark 6 in a roasting tin. Add 2 tbsp tomato puree, roast for 40 minutes till bones and vegetables take on a good brown colour. Place bones and vegetables in a pan of cold water, simmer 3-4 hours. Strain through a sieve. Use liquid only. Reduce to ⅓ quantity. Add two measures of port to a very hot pan, flame off alcohol, add 1 tbsp redcurrant jelly, add stock (jus). Bring to the boil, remove from heat, check seasoning.

6. For the compote, finely dice the shallots and cook without colouring in ½oz of butter. Add a few sprigs of thyme and rosemary. De-vein and chop basil leaves, add to shallots. Add chopped garlic and white wine. Add whole cherry tomatoes. Mix well. Season with black pepper, salt and a pinch of sugar to bring out the flavours. Simmer gently until the tomato skins begin to split.

To Serve

Pour jus over the base of the plate, slice lamb, layer over the jus. Serve coulis in ramekin on side of plate. (Serves 4)

Shortbread Tartlet filled with a Bailey's Ganache set on a Raspberry Coulis

Ingredients

For the Shortbread :
4oz butter unsalted
4oz caster sugar
12oz plain flour
1 egg yolk

For the Ganache :
2oz butter unsalted
2oz white chocolate
10fl oz double cream
2 measures of Bailey's Irish Cream

For the Coulis :
3oz caster sugar
10oz raspberries
10fl oz water
Reserve 3oz raspberries to garnish

Method

For the shortbread: cream the butter and sugar together, fold in flour until thoroughly mixed. Add egg yolk and leave to rest in fridge for 1 hour. Roll out to fit 4 x 3½" tartlet tin (with removable base). Bake in the oven at 170°C/325°F/gas mark 3 for 8-10 minutes (do not allow to colour).

For the ganache: place all ingredients in a double boiler. Slowly melt all ingredients until the mixture becomes smooth, remove from the heat, cool if required.

For the coulis: bring to the boil all ingredients. Simmer for 10-15 minutes. Puree in a food processor, pass through a fine sieve. Cool.

To Serve

Place one tablespoon of coulis in centre of serving plate, and rotate to cover the base of serving plate with the coulis. Remove tartlet from case. Pipe ganache using a star shaped nozzle into tartlet case. Place a raspberry in centre of ganache. The tartlet should then be placed to one side of the serving plate on top of the raspberry coulis. Garnish with remaining raspberries. Dust with icing sugar. Serve immediately. (Serves 4-6)

The Green Inn
Starter

The Green Inn
Main Course

The Green Inn
Pudding

The Lairhillock
Starter

The Lairhillock
Prawns

The Lairhillock
Pudding

My husband Chris and I recently spent a Saturday night here, to celebrate his birthday. We'd had a most frantic day with the children: the usual rugby, dancing and swimming. We left home thoroughly harassed even though our wonderful friend and sitter, Mhairi was smoothing over the chaos. We arrived at Craigellachie late, wondering why we'd bothered, but we were greeted warmly and offered a welcome drink - thank goodness someone had the right idea! We were then treated to the most enjoyable meal we have had in a very long time, with and excellent, faultless service. Mr Tillbury the head chef has really captured the atmosphere of the Speyside area, making the most of local ingredients. Try the Herring in Oatmeal with Grape Chutney and Bacon Salad, this is so good!

A walk up Speyside early next morning before breakfast refreshed both of us. But my husband drew the line at the local haggis and scrambled egg for breakfast on our return! I loved it!!

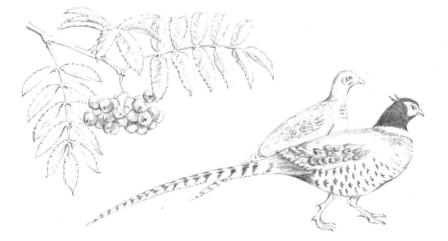

Starter

Herring in Oatmeal with Grape Chutney and Bacon Salad

Ingredients

4 herrings weighing about 225g (8oz) each (filleted)
100g (4oz) oatmeal (fine pinhead)
25ml (1floz) olive oil
4 rashers streaky bacon, cut into thin strips
50g (2oz) mixed salad leaves
2 fresh plum tomatoes (seeded and chopped)
50ml (2floz) basic vinaigrette
Milled sea salt
Freshly ground white pepper

Grape Chutney:
250g grapes (skinned and deseeded)
250g apples (peeled and cored, preferably Cox's)
140g soft brown sugar
62g sultanas
75ml cider vinegar
35ml lemon
Grated zest ¼ lemon
¼ tsp allspice
¼ tsp cloves
¼ tsp sea salt
¼ tsp cinnamon
Pinch paprika
(simmer all ingredients together for 1 hour. Cool and store in a sterilised Kilner jar, this will keep 2 weeks in the refrigerator).
Method

Season and coat the herring fillets with oatmeal, heat olive oil in a nonstick pan and fry the streaky bacon until crispy. Remove and keep warm. Fry the herrings using the same oil until golden brown on both sides. Keep warm.

Dress the salad leaves with vinaigrette and toss the tomato, warm bacon and seasoning. Arrange salad on the serving plates with the warmed herring on top and the grape chutney to one side. Serve immediately. (Serves 4)

Main Course

Casserole of Pheasant and Malt Whisky

Ingredients

1 pheasant, breast and legs removed from carcass
½ pint stock made from carcass and giblets of the pheasant
1½oz unsalted butter
3½ tablespoons olive oil
1½oz plain flour
12oz streaky bacon
8 shallots peeled
2 cloves garlic
5 sprigs thyme
2 bay leaves
8oz mushrooms, field or wild
6fl oz malt whisky
1½oz salted butter, softened
Salt and freshly ground white pepper

Method

Marinade pheasant in 4fl oz whisky with 2 tablespoons olive oil and 3 sprigs of thyme for 6 hours or overnight.

Make a stock from the carcass and drumsticks. Remove the pheasant and thyme from marinade, pat dry with kitchen towel and dust in flour. Sauté the pheasant in the remainder of the olive oil and butter until golden brown, then flame with whisky. Transfer into a large casserole dish.

Using the remaining fat, fry the shallots until golden brown. Dice the bacon into 1½" cubes and fry, reserve with shallots.

Add the remaining thyme and bay leaves to the pheasant and chopped garlic, pour in stock and bring to gentle simmer. Keep on low heat to simmer and cook for 45 minutes.

Add mushrooms (whole), bacon and onions, stir in and simmer for a further 45 minutes, to thicken sauce, or until pheasant is tender and cooked (test with skewer). (Serves 4)

Iced Glayva and Heather Honey Soufflé with Raspberry Coulis

Ingredients

For Soufflé :
4 eggs - separated
4oz caster sugar
¼ pint double cream
1 measure Glayva
1 tablsp heather honey

For Coulis :
300g raspberries
100g caster sugar
Touch of lemon juice
Dash of malt whisky

Method

Line 4 (2 x 2 ½") rings or ramekin dishes with greaseproof paper. Whisk the egg yolks with 2oz of caster sugar, Glayva, and honey until pale in colour and quite thick. Start to whisk the egg whites until half risen, then gradually add in the remaining 2oz of caster sugar whisk until stiff. Whip cream to the soft peaks stage. Using a rubber spatula fold the egg whites very gently into the egg yolk mixture, then fold in the whipped cream. Pipe the mixture into the prepared rings and place in freezer overnight.

For the coulis: mix all the ingredients together, and set aside for 2 hours to allow the flavours to combine. Purée in a food processor, and finally pass through a fine sieve.

To serve: remove soufflé from mould and paper and place on the centre of serving plate. Drizzle coulis around and garnish with sprigs of mint and fresh raspberries. (Serves 4)

FARADAY'S

When I received the recipes from Faraday's, I thought that John Inches, the proprietor, had gone bananas! John has provided us with three courses featuring bananas, which not only look good, but taste delicious. They have also photographed beautifully, which delighted us.

Faraday's has been converted from a former Edwardian pumping station, into an intimate and comfortable home of fine cuisine, providing a sophisticated venue, where everyone gets a personal and welcoming service.

John and his staff work hard to maintain very high standards of food and presentation. The menu is varied, with strong Scottish overtones, his well-travelled palate and creativity are most evident in the menu he has provided.

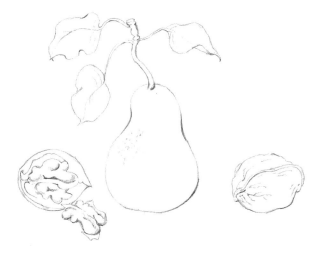

Curried Banana Soup

Ingredients

2oz butter
6 ripe bananas (preferably black free)
2 medium onions chopped
1 red chilli chopped
2 tsps Madras curry paste
1 tsp turmeric
1 lemon juiced
2 pints of good chicken stock
¼ pint single cream
Coriander or parsley to garnish

N.B. - Creamed coconut can also be added to give a milder taste if preferred.

Method

Melt the butter in a pan and sweat off the onion for 5 minutes. Stir in curry paste, chilli and turmeric till amalgamated. Then add the lemon juice, bananas, chicken stock. Bring to the boil and simmer gently for 15 minutes.

Process the soup in a blender till very smooth. Stir in cream, adjust seasoning. Serve with garnish. (Serves 4-6)

Shoulder Steak cooked in Dark Ground Coffee, with Green Bananas and Roasted Chestnuts

Ingredients

2½ lb of shoulder steak (diced into large cubes) and well floured
2 green chillies
3 onions chopped
4 cloves of garlic chopped
4fl oz cooking oil
2 pints of dark ground coffee (filtered)
½ tsp of Burdall's gravy salt
6 green bananas
½ lb fresh chestnuts (peeled)
½ lb shallots (peeled and halved)
Sour cream, chopped bananas, parsley and pilaf rice to garnish

Method

Heat a little vegetable oil in a large frying pan and when very hot add the floured steak to stiffen and brown. When all the meat is browned place in a small casserole. Thereafter brown the onions, then add to the casserole with the meat.

Place the casserole on a moderate heat on top of the stove and add the chillies, garlic, coffee stock and gravy salt. Let this come to the boil and simmer for 2½ hours, till the meat is tender (the cooking time can vary). Roughly ½ hour before end of cooking time cut the bananas into thirds and add to the casserole, simmer very gently.

Meanwhile heat a little oil in a frying pan and stir fry the shallots with the chestnuts till lightly caramelised.

To serve the dish, place the casseroled meat into individual 'sur le plat' dishes, place the caramelised shallots and chestnuts on top and finish the dish with sour cream, chopped banana and parsley. (See picture).

Chef's Tip :

If the casserole appears to be too thin in consistency for personal liking, just add a little plain flour whisked through water and added, to thicken the casserole. Bring back to the boil before serving. (Serves 4-6)

Banana Cake with Raspberry and Pernod Cardinale

Ingredients

For the Cake :
4oz butter
10oz caster sugar
2 eggs
3 tablsps milk
1 tablsp vinegar (mix this with the milk)
1 tsp bicarbonate soda
8oz self-raising flour
3 very ripe bananas (mashed)

For the Cardinale :
8oz raspberries (fresh or frozen)
2oz caster sugar
2fl oz pernod

For the Decoration :
4fl oz whipping cream (lightly whipped)
2 bananas sliced
Juice of ½ lemon (to stop discoloration)
Toasted flaked almonds or pralines

Method

For the Cake :
Cream butter and sugar together until light and fluffy. Add eggs one at a time and beat. Mix bicarbonate of soda with milk/vinegar solution until dissolved. Add to mixture, and beat for 2-3 minutes. Add bananas and beat. Fold in sieved flour. Bake in a lined roasting or cake tin for 35 minutes at 180°C/350°F/gas mark 4. Cool on a wire rack, with a damp tea towel over till cold.

For the Cardinale :
Simply add all ingredients to liquidiser, and process for 2 minutes. Rub through a sieve and rest sauce.

To complete :

Cut a rectangle of banana cake about 8cm x 12cm. Slice into three layers and put some sliced banana with whipped cream on each layer. Finish with either flaked almonds or pralines.

Put a well of the cardinale in the centre of the plate, and place the banana cake in the centre of the well. Dust the edge of the plate with icing sugar and serve. (Serves 4-6)

FARLEYER HOUSE HOTEL

This most delightful Country House Hotel, is set amidst thirty acres of gardens, in the heart of the Tay Valley.

There are nineteen bedrooms in the hotel, with additional rooms in the Ghillies' and Keepers' Cottages in the grounds offering luxury accommodation. I wonder what the previous inhabitants would make of these luxury conversions? Farleyer has secured some of the best salmon fishing on the River Tay, and operates highly-acclaimed Spey casting courses!

The Bistro offers imaginative Scottish cooking in a relaxed, informal atmosphere. The set menu in the Menzies Restaurant, makes the most of the outstanding quality of local game, meat and fish. Head Chef Richard Lyth has certainly provided us with a menu to match any hotel in the area.

House-Cured Gravadlax

Ingredients

1 x 1.5kg side smoked salmon (trimmed & pinboned)
200g Maldon or sea salt crystals
200g caster sugar
Zest of 2 lemons
Zest of 2 oranges
1 tsp chopped fennel seed
3tsp Dijon mustard
2 bunches pickled & chopped dill

Method

Combine salt, sugar, zests and fennel seeds. Smother flesh side of salmon with this mix. Cover and refrigerate. After 24 hours turn salmon so that the flesh is facing down. (The marinade will turn into liquid, this is the salt /sugar curing the salmon.) Refrigerate for a further 24 hours. Rinse salmon in fresh water, removing all traces of the marinade. Dry well, smear all over with the mustard and press chopped dill all over. Slice thinly and serve with lemon and/or mustard dill dressing. (Serves 8-10)

Main Course

Croustiallant of Spiced Perthshire Lamb with Honey and Thyme Sauce

Ingredients

4 x 100g fully trimmed lamb fillets
200g clarified butter
8 sheets filo pastry
Spinach leaves
40g Lexia raisins
60g pine kernels
80g Cairnsmore cheese
Salt
Ground white pepper
Ground coriander
Ground cumin

For the Garnish
400g courgettes, cut into fine strips
2 punnets cherry tomatoes
Olive oil

For the Sauce
570 ml lamb stock
1 tablsp honey
2 tablsp lemon juice
2 tablsp finely chopped thyme
30g cubed butter

Method

Fry and seal lamb fillets in clarified butter. Allow to cool. Butter a sheet of filo pastry and fold to fit individual gratin dish. Place a layer of spinach followed by cheese, pine kernels and raisins. Slice lamb fillet and fan place over layered ingredients. Season with salt, pepper, coriander and cumin. Repeat the raisins, pine kernels, cheese and spinach. Fold over pastry and seal with melted butter. Use the other sheet for decoration. Repeat process for other three dishes. Bake at 180°C/350°F/gas mark 4 for 8-10 minutes. Reduce lamb stock to a quarter of its volume. Add honey, lemon juice and thyme. Then add the butter, melting one cube at a time. Keep sauce warm. Quickly fry the julienned courgettes and the cherry tomatoes.
Place the parcels on warmed plates surrounded by the sauce and garnish with the fried vegetables. (serves 4)

Lemon Gratin with Orange Sauce

Ingredients

190ml lemon juice and zest (6-8 lemons)
100ml cream
6 egg yolks
6 egg whites
340g (+50g) sugar
3 tablsp flour
3 gelatine leaves
8 oranges
100g butter
50ml Grand Marnier
50g icing sugar

Method

Mix the egg yolks with 80g sugar add the flour. Boil the lemon juice, zest and cream. Add to the yolk mixture and bring almost back to boil. Have gelatine already soft and in some water. Drain and add to hot cream. Cook remainder of sugar (260g) with a little water to 118°C. Whisk whites to a snow and continue whisking, while pouring on the sugar syrup. Beat until cold. Fold the cream and meringue together and pour into prepared moulds. Refrigerate. Peel and segment 4 oranges. Juice the other 4 oranges. Bring juice to boil with 50g of sugar, reduce a little and thicken with butter. Place de-moulded gratins on plate, dust with icing sugar and glaze. Surround with orange segments and pour over orange butter. (Serves 6)

THE GLENEAGLES HOTEL

When Gleneagles opened in 1924 it was described as a 'Riviera in the Highlands'. Today it remains dedicated to excellence, just as it was in those early days. It holds the Automobile Association's supreme accolade of five red stars.

Gleneagles nestles in the hills around Auchterarder, Perthshire, in calm and tranquil beauty, but you cannot fail to be impressed, when you turn that final corner, to see the magnificent building of the hotel standing before you.

At the hotel we were received quietly and efficiently, and allowed a choice of location, for the food photography. After this we were placed in the capable hands of junior sous chef Philip Scott, who created a stunning starter and main course for us. We then had the pleasure of meeting Darren Ridley, pastry chef, who astonished us with his most creative dessert - just look at pictures! We had so much fun finding 'props', it's amazing what you can find in the golf shop. The Gleneagles experience, most certainly does not stop with the sumptuous food. Golf would certainly come higher on my husband's list of priorities. This I can understand, when you have three 18-hole championship courses and one 9-hole to choose from. They are truly magnificent. Other sporting opportunities abound: clay pigeon shooting, all-weather tennis, swimming, squash, croquet, fishing, falconry, off-road driving and horse-riding.

A wonderful break and what an experience!

Potted Scallop and Salmon with Whisky Mustard Vinaigrette

Ingredients

6 scallops
4oz cooked flaked salmon
4fl oz heavy cream
½ egg white
½ lemon juice
1 tsp dill chopped
8oz puff pastry
Egg wash

For the Vinaigrette :
4fl oz olive oil
2 tsp grain mustard
2 tsp whisky
Spring onions (finely sliced)
Squeeze lemon juice

4 bunches of mixed salad leaves

Method

1. Place the scallops in a blender with the egg white and a pinch of salt and puree, slowly add the cream blending on pulse. Do not over mix or the cream will curdle.

2. Put the flaked salmon into a bowl with the chopped dill, and lemon juice and bind with the scallop mousse, adjust seasoning.

3. Spoon the mixture into four buttered 2½" ramekin moulds. Leave to rest for 1 hour in fridge.

4. Roll out the puff pastry, cut into circles ¼" larger than the ramekin. Egg wash and place on top of the filled moulds, again leave for at least 1 hour.

5. Mix all ingredients together for the vinaigrette and season.

6. Cook the salmon/scallop mousses in a Bain-marie at 200°C/ 400°F/ gasmark 6 for 15-20 minutes.

7. Make a nest of leaves in the middle of the plate and place the mousse on top and sauce around the vinaigrette. (See picture). (Serves 4)

Highland Venison Saddle with Pickled Plums and Sweet Red Cabbage

Ingredients

600g venison saddle
2 plums
25g black peppercorns
1 cinnamon stick
25g castor sugar
50ml balsamic vinegar
150g puff pastry
400g red cabbage
60ml red wine

60ml redcurrant jelly
Pinch of salt and pepper
160g French beans
200g carrots
150ml game jus (stock)
30ml port
155g butter unsalted
30g shallots
4 tbsp olive oil

Method

1.   Add the sugar and peppercorns to the balsamic vinegar. Heat gently to dissolve sugar then boil rapidly until reduced by half. Add cinnamon stick and sliced wedges of plums to the liquid and leave to pickle for half a day.

2.   Finely shred the red cabbage, place some oil in a pan and add the cabbage and cook. When soft add the red wine and reduce by half then add redcurrant jelly and finish cooking and season.

3.   Peel carrots, chop and place in a separate pan. Cover with salted water and cook until soft. Drain well and place in a food processor and purée.

4.   Take the French beans and top and tail them so they are all the same length, then blanch and refresh.

5.   Remove plums from pickling juices and dry. Roll out puff pastry thinly and cut out a 4cm disc and arrange the plums into the pastry discs. Then place onto a tray with silicone paper underneath and place into fridge for 20 minutes to rest.

6.   Pre-heat the oven to 200°C/400°F/gas mark 6. For the sauce, shred the shallots and lightly sweat them in a pan until soft. Add port and reduce, add game jus and reduce until required consistency is achieved.

7.   Add some oil to a frying pan, season the venison loin and place in the hot pan. Seal the meat on all sides and place in the oven for 8-10 minutes depending on how well you like your meat cooked. Place the plum tart, in the oven, to cook with the venison.

8.   While the meat is cooking re-heat the cabbage, carrot puree, beans, and sauce. Remove the tart when cooked. When venison is cooked, remove from the oven and rest for a few minutes.

9.   When all the vegetables are hot, season and place the cabbage on one side of the plate following the curve of the plate round. On the opposite side place the tart and the beans below, and on top of the beans place a quenelle of carrot purée. (See picture)

10.   Bring the sauce to the boil then whisk in a knob of butter to finish the sauce and check the seasoning. Slice four to five pieces of the venison and place onto the cabbage, then pour sauce around, and serve. (Serves 4)

Berry Parfait

Ingredients

500ml cream (whipped)
120gm egg yolks
50gm sugar
100gm slightly broken berries

Method

1. Whip the egg yolks and sugar until thick (ribbon stage). Then fold into the whipped cream with the broken berries. Set aside.

2. Lightly dust a strip of plastic with cocoa powder, then smooth some tempered white chocolate or chocolate coating on top. Allow to set a little and bend round (with the chocolate on the inside).

3. When the chocolate has set, pipe on the parfait mixture and freeze.

4. Serve as seen with blueberry compôte.

Tuille

Ingredients

100gm flour
100gm butter
100gm egg white
100gm icing sugar

Method

1. Mix the melted butter, icing sugar and flour into a smooth paste and add the egg white.

2. Leave in the fridge for approximately 1 hour and spread onto a silicone paper mat.

3. Bake at 180°C/350°F/gas mark 4 until golden brown and then bend into shape while still hot.

Sugar Springs

Ingredients

500gm sugar
250ml water
Pinch of tartar

Method

1. Boil sugar and water until caramelised and allow to cool a little

2. Dip spoon into the sugar and pull it away from the pan so that it forms a strand. Wrap the strand of sugar around a knife, sharpening steel or metal tube. When cool remove.

Blueberry Compôte

Ingredients

1kg frozen blueberries
500gm sugar

Method

1. Cook the sugar and blueberries together until thick, allow to cool and serve. Assemble as seen in picture. (Serves 4)

The restaurant is perfectly placed on the village green in the heart of Ballater. Jeff and Carol Purves have been running the business since 1980, to great acclaim throughout the Deeside area. They are very genuine, hard-working people. I am extremely grateful to Jeff for all the time he spent helping me with suggestions and photographs for the book. The Purves work very much as a team, Jeff in the kitchen and Carol 'out front.' They have created that very fine balance required in both areas, which satisfies customers so that they cannot fail to return.

Jeff prepares all the food on the premises, with maximum use being made of local fresh produce. Only free-range eggs are used, game is from local moors and forests, venison is always wild and all fish and shellfish are fresh not frozen. The preservation of the environment is important to Jeff: with this in mind, he only cooks male lobsters and diver-caught scallops. Traditional Scottish specialities always feature regularly on the menu.

Vegetarian food is also given due consideration by Jeff, who advises pre-booking, to allow him to do justice to your requirements. I was not surprised to discover a string of awards for the restaurant. The AA has given two rosettes for food. They won The Taste of Scotland MacAllan Award Restaurant of the Year in 1995. In 'The Good Food Guide' Jeff's cooking is rated as highly as that of Nick Nairn, and Ballater is nearer for some than Glasgow.

Oaksmoked Haddock Topped with Roasted Cheese on a Tomato Salsa

Ingredients

4 medium size oak-smoked haddock
4oz mature cheddar
4 tomatoes, blanched, seeds and skin removed and diced
1 lime, juice and grated rind
1 spring onion diced
1 very small pinch of cayenne pepper
¼oz salt flakes

Method

1. Dice the tomatoes and mix with the lime juice, cayenne pepper, spring onion and salt flakes in a glass bowl. Leave to stand for 30 minutes.

2. Place haddock in buttered earthware dish and top with cheese. Roast in oven 190°C/375°F/gas mark 5 for 8 minutes.

3. Place tomato salsa onto 4 plates and place the haddock on top to serve. (Serves 4)

Main Course

Pan fried Wild Boar Cutlet with Roast Loin of Venison and Walnut Sauce

Ingredients

Potatoes :
150g Duchesse mix potatoes
4 (2 x ½" potato circles)
Coarse salt
Oil for frying
Rice flour for dusting potatoes

Venison Loin :
200g middle cut wild venison loin
Olive oil
2 bay leaves
1 bunch thyme
6 juniper berries

Walnut Sauce :
100g crushed walnuts
50g chopped shallot
190ml dry Madeira
560ml veal jus-lie/stock
380ml chicken stock
60ml walnut oil

Stir Fry of Vegetables :
30g julienne mange-tout
30g julienne courgettes
30g julienne straw mushrooms
10g finely chopped ginger
Salt and pepper

Wild Boar :
4 x 100g wild boar cutlets
Salt and pepper

Chanterelles :
8 medium Chanterelles dry and free from dirt & grit
Butter
Salt

Timbale of Butternut Squash with Parsley Sauce :
120g diced butternut squash
¼ clove crushed garlic
380ml béchamel/white sauce
300g chopped parsley
190ml single cream
30g butter
Salt and pepper
Nutmeg

Method

1. Marinade venison in olive oil, thyme, bay leaves and juniper berries for 6 hours.

2. Blanch potato rounds in salt water for 10 minutes, drain.

3. Shape Duchesse potatoes into 4 cakes. Colour quickly on both sides. Brush with melted butter.

4. Blanch butternut squash for 3 minutes, drain and season with salt, pepper, nutmeg and garlic. Bind with 25ml béchamel - keep warm.

5. Sweat shallots in a little butter, do not colour. Add walnuts, Madeira and chicken stock. Reduce by half. Add veal jus-lie, reduce to coating consistency. Check seasoning, strain and keep hot.

6. Bring béchamel and single cream to the boil, reduce to a good thick cream, add chopped parsley. Adjust seasoning, cover to prevent skin forming. Keep warm.

7. Drain venison of marinade. Pan fry on both sides, season with salt and pepper and roast at 200°C/400°F/gas mark 6 for 8 minutes. Must be underdone. Rest and keep warm.

8. Pan fry boar cutlet on both sides (medium). Season with salt and pepper. Rest and keep warm.

9. Colour potato rounds on both sides, season with salt. Place in oven to continue cooking.

10. Place potato cakes in oven to heat through.

11. Bind butter squash with 190ml parsley sauce. Place in round 2½" cutter on bottom left-hand corner of warm plate, and top with remaining parsley sauce.

12. Stir fry vegetables and straw mushrooms, season with ginger, salt and pepper. Place on top right-hand corner of warm plate.

13. Place potato circle on stir fry.

14. Put the potato cake on top left-hand of plate.

15. Warm wild boar cutlet and place on top of stir fry and potato.

16. Warm loin of venison and slice into 12 slices. Place 3 slices overlapping the bottom of the boar cutlet.

17. Quickly sauté chanterelles, season with salt and pepper, place in bottom right-hand of plate.

18. Reheat sauce, whisk in walnut oil, Adjust seasoning. Do not boil. Flood plates with sauce. Remove cutters and serve. (Serves 4)

Raspberry Gratins

Ingredients

3 lemons rind and juice
1 sheet of leaf gelatine
3fl oz double cream
3 eggs
4oz sugar

½oz arrowroot
1lb raspberries
2oz castor sugar
3floz red wine

Method

Pick over raspberries and keep 8oz of the best for presentation. Puree the rest with red wine and 2oz caster sugar, then strain. Lightly grease 4 (3 x 1½") rings and clingfilm the bottom to hold in position, place on a tray.

1. Dissolve lemon juice, and add rind to the arrowroot.

2. Soak gelatine leaf for 20 minutes.

3. Boil cream then add lemon juice and arrowroot, re-boil, cool. Beat in 3 yolks while mixture is still warm.

4. Beat egg whites stiff with 4oz castor sugar.

5. Fold egg white mixture into lemon mixture. Place into greased rings. Place in fridge for minimum of 1 hour.

6. Remove clingfilm from rings, place on plate, sprinkle with icing sugar and glaze under very hot grill.

7. Place in fridge to set.

8. Arrange raspberries around ring.

9. Flood plate with raspberry sauce.

10. Remove rings and serve. (Serves 4)

KINLOCH LODGE

On the Hebridean Island of Skye, well known for the challenging mountain climbing in the Cuillins, hillwalking, fishing and many other outdoor pursuits, Lord and Lady MacDonald established Kinloch Lodge, as their family home and turned it into a small country hotel in 1973. Over the last 25 years Lady MacDonald has become a well-known creative food writer and expert in her field. She has written numerous cookery books and won the prestigious Glenfiddich Award for one of them. Her own unique style is founded upon the use of the freshest and most natural ingredients from the gardens, moors and waters of Skye, this has become her trademark.

The lodge gives the appearance and retains the feeling of a relaxed, comfortable family home. Chris and I first stayed at Kinloch Lodge one Easter to go hill walking, eat good food and stop me pining for Scotland, we lived in London at the time. My most recent visit was to a three-day cookery course at Kinloch Lodge. Lady MacDonald demonstrated the food, which we later ate in the restaurant. A blissfull three days!

Most recently the 'Claire MacDonald Centre' of food and cookery has been built in the grounds, at the side of the lodge. This is now open and will accommodate more cookery demonstrations and visitors.

Herb Crêpes with Smoked Salmon and Cucumber

Ingredients

2 large eggs
4oz plain flour
Fresh herbs, any or all of: parsley, snipped chives, chervil, dill, about a
handful of herbs in total
½ pint milk and 2 tablespoons water
1oz butter, melted
Salt and pepper

For the Filling:
½ lb smoked salmon, cut into fairly fine dice
½ pint crème fraîche
½ cucumber, skinned, deseeded, and diced finely
Black pepper

Method

To make the crêpes, (the batter for which can be made a day in advance and kept in the fridge), put the eggs into a food processor and whizz, gradually adding the flour, milk and water, and melted butter. Whizz in the herbs - snip the chives first - add the salt and pepper. Leave this batter to stand for at least 30 minutes before making it up into crêpes. Stir it well before using. Make into crêpes by melting a small amount of butter in a crêpe pan, then pour in a small amount of batter, swirling it around in the hot pan so that it forms a thin film over the bottom of the crêpe pan.

Cook for a few seconds, then with your fingertips uppermost and thumbs under the crêpe, flip it over to cook on its other side for a few seconds. Slip the cooked crêpe onto a plastic tray to cool, or a cloth covered board (they stick to wood) and repeat the process. When cold, stack the crêpes with a strip of baking parchment between each. Make them in the morning for dinner that same day.

To assemble, mix together the ingredients for the filling. Put a spoonful- a generous one!- on one half of each crêpe. Fold the other half over, to form a half-moon shape, and put two of these on each plate, straight sides together so that they form a whole. I put a sprig of dill between the two. The herbs give a bright fresh colour to the crêpes, as well as enhancing their flavour. (Serves 8)

Spinach and Parmesan Stuffed Chicken with Saffron Sauce

Ingredients

6 chicken breasts, without their skins, and all bones removed
2 cloves garlic, skinned and chopped
4oz fresh spinach
2oz grated fresh parmesan
A good grating of nutmeg
Juice of 2 lemons
2 tablespoons olive oil

For the Sauce :
3 tablespoons olive oil
1 large or 2 small /medium onions, skinned and very neatly chopped
1 pint good chicken stock
5fl oz double cream
½ teaspoon saffron strands
Salt and pepper

Method

Put the spinach, garlic, parmesan and grated nutmeg into a food processor and whizz, adding half the lemon juice. Lay the chicken breasts on a board and flatten as much as you can. Spread the spinach mixture thinly over each, and roll or fold in half and stick a wooden toothpick through each, or tie with string or cotton. Put the chicken breasts into an ovenproof dish and pour the rest of the lemon juice over them, plus 2 tablespoons olive oil. Bake for 40-45 minutes in a moderate oven-180°C/ 350°F, gas mark 4.

To make the sauce - do this in a sauté pan for speed - heat the oil and cook the finely-chopped onion in the oil for several minutes till well softened and turning golden brown. Soak the saffron in the stock and then pour this into the onions. Let it simmer and reduce by about half in quantity. Pour in the cream and let the sauce bubble for a couple of minutes. Season with salt and pepper. Take the toothpicks out of the cooked chicken or cut off the string or cotton before dishing up. Serve each chicken breast with spoonfuls of sauce over and around. (Serves 6)

Lemon and Vanilla Soufflés

I love the combined flavours of lemon and vanilla. These soufflés make delicious eating for a special lunch or dinner-time pudding. They are convenient to prepare because you can make them in their entirety, including folding in the whisked whites, then cover the whole lot with clingfilm, get washed up, and leave the soufflés for a couple of hours. Whip off the clingfilm before putting them into the oven to cook. But, as with all soufflés, they must be eaten immediately - dust with icing sugar, which you have all ready with the spoon and sieve.

Ingredients

5 large eggs, separated
5oz/170g caster sugar
Grated rind of 2 well-washed and dried lemons
Juice of 1 lemon
A few drops of vanilla extract, ½ tsp essence
2oz/56g ground almonds, sieved
Butter and icing sugar
6 large ramekins

Method

Butter the ramekins and dust them out with icing sugar. Whisk the egg yolks, gradually adding the sugar and whisking till the mousse-like mixture is very pale and thick. Whisk in the lemon rinds and juice, the vanilla and the ground almonds. In a separate bowl, with clean whisks, whisk the whites till they are stiff. With a large metal spoon fold them quickly and thoroughly through the lemon mixture.

Divide evenly between the prepared ramekins. Bake in a moderate oven, 350°F/180°C/gas mark 4 for 25 minutes. Dust each with icing sugar and serve immediately, with a bowl of whipped cream or with sieved raspberry purée if you prefer, or with both. (Serves 6)

THE LAIRHILLOCK

The Lairhillock was once a small coaching inn on the old Aberdeen to Stonehaven road. Although coaches no longer pull up at its doors, the inn is alive with people from Aberdeen, and the surrounding area. People enjoy the short drive along the South Deeside road into the countryside to sample the delights on the menu in the country pub and restaurant.

Extensive refurbishment has been carried out by the owners, Frank and Anne Budd, to maintain a rustic appeal throughout. The low ceilings and open hearth with log fire create a very cosy, relaxed atmosphere for which The Lairhillock is well known.

Chef Hermann Schmid has recently arrived at The Lairhillock. The food he prepared for us was extremely creative and, as you will read in the chocolate mousse recipe, every mouthful is worth fighting over.

Warm Chargrilled Salmon Salad with Citrus Fruit with a Honey and Shallot Vinaigrette

Ingredients

For the Vinaigrette :
2 tablsp English mustard
4 tablsp cider vinegar
5 shallots, finely diced
¼ litre olive oil
⅓ litre vegetable oil
3 tablsp clear honey
Salt, pepper and chopped parsley
Water

For the Salmon and Citrus Fruit :
8 slices of fresh salmon fillet (thinly sliced)
Salt, pepper and lemon juice
2 grapefruits (segmented)
3 oranges (segmented)
Mixed lettuce leaves of iceberg, radiccio and curly endive
Chives (chopped)
Fresh basil (chopped)

Method

1. For the vinaigrette whisk the English mustard and the cider vinegar and slowly add the olive oil until it is of thick consistency. Add a little water and more olive oil if required. Add shallot, honey and chopped parsley. Season with salt and pepper.

2. Arrange the mixed lettuce leaves, chopped chives and basil in a soup plate. Pour over some vinaigrette.

3. Season salmon with salt and pepper, squeeze fresh lemon juice over fillets.

4. Using a very hot griddle pan, sear the salmon for 30 seconds on each side, arrange over the mixed lettuce leaves. Arrange citrus fruits on top. Pour over more vinaigrette. Crispy bacon or croutons can be added if you wish to do so. (Serves 4)

Sautéed King Scallops and Langoustine Tails with a Champagne, Spinach and Mustard Cream, served with a Sweet Pepper Risotto Wrapped in Smoked Salmon and Garnished with Deep Fried Root Ginger

Ingredients

12 large whole langoustines
8 fresh king scallops in the shell
Clarified butter
Flour and seasoning
4 slices smoked salmon
**see method for other ingredients*

This is one of Chef Hermann Schmid's most sought after main courses. Many people order a fish starter and main course these days because of healthier eating habits!

Method

Peel langoustines. Keep shells for stock. Put fresh scallops in a hot oven until they pop open. Remove and rinse with cold water. Loosen scallops from shell and clean. Keep aside four shells for presentation.

1. Shell fish stock: langoustine shells, 1 carrot, 1 celery stick, 1 bayleaf, 1 diced onion, 1 teaspoon black pepper corns and ½ pint of water. Bring all the ingredients to the boil in a heavy based pan. Reduce heat and cook for a further 50 minutes. Reduce to ⅓ pint.

2. Risotto: 200-250g. long grain rice, 1 medium diced onion, ½ each diced red and green pepper, 1 clove garlic crushed, 500g vegetable stock, 1 teaspoon turmeric, salt and pepper to taste. Sauté onions, peppers and garlic. Add rice, turmeric, and vegetable stock. Season and cook until ready. The risotto can be prepared in advance and reheated in the oven or microwave.

3. The champagne, spinach and mustard sauce: 2oz leaf spinach cut into strips, 2 oz chopped shallots, 10fl oz double cream, 2oz clarified butter, 2 teaspoon mild mustard, shell fish stock, 1 glass champagne, or a good dry sparkling wine, 1 teaspoon flour. Sauté shallots in the butter until soft. Add flour, stock, champagne and cream. Reduce to a creamy texture. Add the mustard and simmer. Lastly, add the spinach. Deep fry strips of fresh root ginger until golden brown. Allow to cool.

4. Season shell fish. Dust with flour and sauté with clarified butter or olive oil in a hot pan for a few minutes on each side. Do not overcook.

5. Press the risotto firmly into a lightly-oiled ramekin or any small oven-proof dish and reheat in a hot oven.

6. Add sautéed shell fish to sauce and reheat. Do not allow to come to the boil.

7. Presentation: Turn risotto out on to a plate and wrap with smoked salmon that has been placed under a high grill for 30 seconds. Fill each shell with 2 scallops, 3 langoustine tails, and garnish risotto with deep fried ginger.

Chef's Tip : To keep scallop shells from moving, put a little risotto or mashed potato on the plate and then place shells on top. (Serves 4)

Starter

Aubergine Paté

Ingredients

1 large aubergine
2 tablsp coarse grain salt
2 tablsp olive oil
2 garlic cloves
4oz chopped tomatoes
1 tablsp tomato paste
8oz Philadelphia cheese
2 tablsp chopped coriander
Seasoning

Method

1. Peel and dice the aubergine, add the coarse salt, put in a colander. Leave for 1 hour, then rinse and drain well.

2. In a wok or large pan, add the olive oil and aubergine and cook for about 10 minutes. Stirring well.

3. Add tomato paste and garlic, cook for a further 5 minutes.

4. Put this mixture in a liquidiser for 2-3 minutes, adding the Philadelphia cheese little by little. Season well then add the chopped coriander.

5. Put in a dish in the fridge overnight. Serve with warm bread. (Serves 6)

Main Course

Maize Fed Chicken with Rhubarb

Ingredients

4 maize fed chicken breasts or
1 x 4lb 5oz. chicken
1lb freshly cut rhubarb
3oz caster sugar
½ glass white wine
2 tbsp chopped shallots
Seasoning
1oz butter

Method

1. Grill the chicken breasts or roast the whole chicken

2. In a pan, add some butter, then the shallots. Stir well on low heat.

3. Add the washed and diced rhubarb, then the caster sugar - stir well for two or three minutes - add white wine and seasoning.

4. You can cook it for 5 minutes or longer depending how you like the rhubarb (with or without chunks).

5. Serve with the chicken. (Serves 4)

Dessert

Tarte Caramelise aux Pommes

Ingredients

15 golden delicious apples
4oz butter unsalted
4oz sugar
1 packet of ready made puff pastry

Method

1. Peel and core the apples. Cut them into small quarters.

2. Melt the butter in a large pan, add the apples. Cook them slowly for 7-8 minutes, add the sugar then cook for a further 4 minutes at a very high heat until the apples start to caramelise. Then drain for 10 minutes in a colander.

3. Place your apples in a "Le Creuset" dish or a butter tray with metal rings.

4. Cook in the oven for 15 minutes at 180°C/350°F/gas mark 4.

5. Let the 'tarte' cool down then cover with puff pastry.

6. Cook in the oven for another 15 minutes.

7. Serve up-side-down on a plate with custard sauce. (Serves 4)

The Marcliffe at Pitfodels on the North Deeside Road is owned by Stewart and Shelia Spence who are members of the Small Luxury Hotels of the World. The atmosphere is luxurious in every respect and great care has been given to the smallest detail. The hotel is now a large modern building tastefully encompassing, the older existing house.

We have enjoyed many a fine evening at the Marcliffe either for dinner or an evening function. There are two restaurants: The Conservatory and the Invery Room, both of which have extensive menus, combining fine Scottish ingredients with modern-style, French influence. Not only is the food of an excellent standard but there are also 100 malt whiskies and 400 wines to choose from.

The head chef, Michael Stoddart, has many accolades to his name and has worked throughout Great Britain and Europe. At a cookery demonstration I recently attended, Lady MacDonald commented on the quality of the food at the Marcliffe. Imagine, 200 for lunch!

Mosaic of Seafoods with Mediterranean Vegetables

Ingredients

1 aubergine sliced - lengthways
1 courgette sliced - lengthways
2 red peppers
2 green peppers
2 yellow peppers
2lb fresh leaf spinach
4oz cocktail prawns
4oz sliced smoked salmon
12 king scallops
1pt tomato juice
1tsp tomato purée
8 basil leaves
¼ clove garlic
100ml white wine
10 leaves gelatine

Method

Blanch spinach leaves in salted water and refresh. Pan fry aubergines and courgettes, season. Roast peppers for 15-20 minutes and peel and remove seeds. In a pan bring to the boil the tomato juice, purée, basil, garlic and white wine, dissolve gelatine in the liquid, leave in fridge to cool down slightly.

Line terrine with cling film and then spinach. Add a little gelatine mixture on the bottom and then spread out the prawns, a little bit more gelatine, the yellow peppers, gelatine, courgette, gelatine, smoked salmon, gelatine, red peppers, gelatine, scallops, gelatine, aubergine, gelatine, green pepper, gelatine. Cover the top with spinach and put in fridge to set. (Serves 8)

Pavé of Halibut with Kedgeree and Topped with a Poached Egg

Ingredients

8oz halibut
4 eggs for poaching

For the Kedgeree :
2oz haddock
2oz basmati rice
4oz good fish stock
1oz chopped shallots
1tsp chopped chives
1tsp curry powder
1 boiled egg

For the Cream Sauce :
½pt fish stock
½pt double cream
1 shallot - chopped
½tsp chopped tarragon
½pt white wine

Method

For the Kedgeree:
Cook rice in the fish stock with the haddock and shallot, add curry powder and allow to simmer. Add hard-boiled egg and chopped chives. For the cream sauce: reduce fish stock with the shallots and white wine, then add cream and reduce by half, check seasoning and add tarragon. Pan fry halibut in olive oil and season, cook in oven. Place kedgeree in middle of plate, put halibut on top with poached egg on top of the halibut. Pour sauce around fish. (Serves 4)

Summer Pudding

Ingredients

80g blueberries
80g raspberries
80g strawberries
10 slices of white bread
200g caster sugar
8fl oz water

Method

Place all the ingredients in a small pan with the sugar and water and cook gently until the fruit is soft but still in shape. Strain the fruit, keeping it separate from its juices. Cut the crusts off the bread - it is better if the bread is a few days old. Place a round shape of bread in the base of a ramekin mould. Then dip strips of bread into the cooled fruit juice and line the mould.

Fill the moulds with the fruit compote and top with another round of bread. Refrigerate overnight. Serve with double cream. (Serves 4)

As you drive out from Aberdeen on the A947 through Oldmeldrum, you have little indication of the glorious sight that awaits you through the gates of Meldrum House Hotel.

The House, a Scottish Baronial Mansion, stands in 12 acres of lawns and woodland, with its own small loch. This tranquil setting hosts many large-scale functions with elegant marquees that overlook the loch. In August Meldrum House opens an 18-hole golf course, eagerly awaited by all enthusiasts in the area, of whom there are many.

Chef Mark Will has created a simple, but inspiring menu for our book, which we are very grateful for. The trout is not from the loch in the grounds, but I have no doubt there is a good source near-by!

Seared Rainbow Trout with Dill Cous Cous on a Mustard Sauce

Ingredients

2 whole rainbow trout
1 tomato
2 sprigs of dill
10oz white cous cous
3oz finely diced onions
1 clove garlic
2fl oz white wine
4oz fresh mussels
Cream
Salt and pepper
14fl oz fish stock
1 tsp wholegrain mustard. Add a touch of whisky

Method

Fillet and clean the trout then season. Blanch the tomato and chop into small diamonds (remove skin, halve and remove flesh and seeds). Set aside.

Chop and sweat off garlic and onions. Add white wine and reduce by half.

Add the washed mussels and cover. When the mussels open, pick out of the shells and put back into the pan with the onions and the garlic, add the cream and mustard to the mussel mixture, reduce by half. Season if required. Stir.

Put fish stock onto the heat and when it starts to simmer add the cous cous and cover, stirring occasionally

Sear the trout in a hot smoking pan for 1 minute each side then transfer to the oven to cook for a further 10 minutes at 180°C/350°F/gas mark 4.

To serve place a spoonful of the cous cous mixture into a small mould in the middle of the plate, remove mould. Place the trout on top. Liquidise the mussel mixture and pass through a sieve then add the tomato diamonds. Pour the sauce around the cous cous. Garnish with deep fried dill. (Serves 4)

Pork and Lamb Battenberg

Ingredients
2 x racks of lamb
2 x pork fillets
1lb sorrel
2lb smoked bacon

Method

Trim fillet of pork. Remove the bones from the rack of lamb, and all the fat, leaving the eye of the meat. Pick and wash sorrel. Place in boiling water for a couple of seconds and then refresh in cold water.

Lay a sheet of clingfilm on the work surface and place the rashers of bacon on top. Then place the blanched sorrel on top of the bacon. Place a pork fillet on the left side of the bacon and sorrel and a rack of lamb on the right. Then do the opposite and place a lamb on top of the pork and then a pork fillet on top of the lamb. Wrap neatly with the bacon.

The final result should then represent the idea of a battenberg cake. Finally fold the right side of the clingfilm tightly over the left and vice versa. Chill overnight. Slice the loaf into the amount of pieces required then pan fry on each side until nice and brown. Ensure the bacon is tightly wrapped round the meat, otherwise it will fall apart. Cook in a hot oven for 5-8 minutes.

For the Gravy

Ingredients
½ pint beef jus/stock
1 measure whisky
2oz finely chopped onions

Method

Heat a frying pan until quite hot and sweat off the onions. Add the whisky and flame. Then pour in the beef jus and bring to the boil. Pass through a sieve and serve. (Serves 4)

Chef's Tip : If you do not chill the dish overnight it will be extremely difficult to cut into portions.

Dessert

Rhubarb Toffee Crumble

Ingredients

For the Sweet Pastry :
10oz plain flour
3oz icing sugar
Pinch of salt
4oz unsalted butter
1 egg
1 tablespoon milk
10oz rhubarb

For the Crumble mix :
8oz plain flour
4oz unsalted butter
4oz caster sugar

1 tin condensed milk

Method

Sieve the flour into a bowl, then rub in the salt and butter. Stir in the sugar and then mix in the egg. Use the milk to mix the pastry to a dough. Place in a bag in the fridge to chill. Place an unopened tin of condensed milk in a pan of water and boil for three hours, topping up the pan with water if necessary. Leave tin to cool then the toffee will be ready. While the tin is boiling use the pastry to line four flan rings. Line the pastry with greaseproof paper and bake blind in the oven for 15-20 minutes. Remove blind baking beans and leave to cool.

Cut the rhubarb into chunks, then place in a saucepan with 2oz soft brown sugar and cook over a gentle heat for 15 minutes. Take the rhubarb off the heat and leave to cool, meanwhile make the crumble mixture. Place the flour in a large mixing bowl then add the butter and rub into the flour using your finger tips. When it resembles fine breadcrumbs add the sugar and mix well. Put rhubarb into pastry cases and top with toffee from the tin. Sprinkle crumble mix on the top. Bake in moderate oven for 15-20 minutes. (Serves 4-6)

Nick Nairn's new restaurant is Glasgow has been a runaway success, so much so that it's really difficult to get a booking. In Braeval, his first restaurant, a new standard of Scottish cooking was set. During this ten year period as a self-taught chef, he has worked hard to change the way we think about and prepare Scottish food. His likeable, energetic personality and enthusiasm for food have earned him a place in the hearts of many as a T.V. chef. His cookery books are widely known. He is also the youngest Scottish chef to earn a Michelin star.

Nairns is the latest endeavour of Nick and his brother, with a great deal of help from his mum, whose eye for décor can be seen in the four bedrooms she designed within the building. It's great when the family is involved in the business, and the necessary creativity and energy is most certainly present in the Nairn family.

At Nairns the aim is to provide affordable glamour. Magic food and special service seven days a week, its almost too good to be true, but at Nairns it's a reality. Book well in advance to avoid disappointment! Eat, be happy and have fun is the message of this restaurant. We are therefore very fortunate to be able to share this experience with you when you try the following recipes!

Wild Mushroom Soup

Ingredients

50g (2oz) unsalted butter
100g (4oz) onion, thinly sliced
1 clove garlic, crushed
450g (1lb) Paris browns (or Chestnut mushrooms)
15g (1 ½oz) dried Ceps (optional)
25ml (1 fl oz) light soy sauce
½ teaspoon salt
5 turns fresh ground white pepper
600ml (1 pint) boiling water
Pinch chives or flat parsley or basil or tarragon
60ml (2½ fl oz) fresh cream

Method

Melt the butter in a large saucepan and gently sweat the onions and garlic for 10 minutes until soft. Add mushrooms (including dried Ceps, if you're using them) and stir to coat. Now add the soy sauce and the seasoning and finally the boiling water.

Bring to the boil, then simmer for 40 minutes until the mushrooms are tender. Liquidise the soup and check the seasoning.

When serving, garnish with a squiggle of cream and some greenery (chives, flat parsley, basil or tarragon), or drop on a few sliced sautéed mushrooms. (Serves 6)

Slow - Roast Chicken Thighs with Spicy Cous Cous

Ingredients

For the Chicken :
4 boned chicken thighs (about 125g/4oz each)
Salt and pepper
2 tablespoons olive oil
1 garlic clove, lightly crushed
1 tablespoon fresh lemon juice

For the Cous Cous :
1 teaspoon ground coriander
1 teaspoon ground cinnamon
½ teaspoon ground cumin
1 tablespoon soft brown sugar
375ml (12fl oz chicken stock)
225g (8oz) cous cous
25g (1oz) raisins
15g (½oz) pine kernels, toasted
3 tablespoons olive oil
1 tablespoon fresh lemon juice
2 tablespoons chopped fresh mint
½oz butter

Method

Season the chicken thighs well on both sides. Heat a frying pan over medium heat. Add the oil and garlic to the pan and then the chicken, skin-side down, and cook for about 20 minutes, until the skin is richly golden and very crisp. Turn the chicken over, discard the garlic and cook for another 2 minutes. Add the lemon juice and shake well to distribute evenly. Cook for 3 minutes and then keep warm.

For the cous cous, melt the butter in a large saucepan. Add the spices and fry gently for 1 minute. Add the sugar and stock and bring to the boil. Pour in the cous cous in a steady stream, stir in the raisins and pine kernels and cover with a tight-fitting lid. Remove from the heat and set aside for about 6-8 minutes to allow the grains to swell up. Then uncover and fork in the olive oil, lemon juice, chopped mint and season to taste.

To serve, carve each chicken thigh into six or seven pieces. Pile the cous cous in the centre of four warmed plates, place the chicken on top. (Serves 4)

Dessert

Plum Clafoutis

Ingredients

75g (3oz) butter
10 ripe victoria plums, halved and stoned
8 medium eggs
225g (8oz) caster sugar, plus extra to serve
½ teaspoon salt
2 tablespoons dark rum
400ml (14fl oz) milk
225g (8oz) plain flour

Method

Pre-heat oven to 200°C/400°F/gas mark 6

Use 25g (1oz) of the butter to grease a round, shallow 28cm (11in) ovenproof dish. Place the plums in the dish cut-side down. Melt the rest of the butter in a small pan.

Break the eggs into a large mixing bowl and add the sugar, salt, rum and milk. Whisk together and then gradually whisk in the flour and the melted butter. Pour the mixture through a sieve into the baking dish and bake for 40 minutes, until well risen and golden brown. Dredge with caster sugar and serve immediately. (Serves 8)

Q Brasserie
Vegetables

Q Brasserie
Main Course

Q Brasserie
Pudding

Q Brasserie
Starter

The Thainstone House Hotel
Main Course

The Thainstone House Hotel
Pudding

THE NOSHEEN TANDOORI RESTAURANT

When in 1989 we heard that an Indian Restaurant was about to open in Ellon, many people (including my parents who were hoteliers) were very surprised. We are still regarded as being "in the country" out here, and the whole project was regarded as an interesting adventure.

The Nosheen has never looked back, and continues to gain popularity. Top quality food and first-class service are a priority. Several very prestigious awards have been won by the restaurant, and it was nominated Patak's restaurant of the year in 1992. The chef specialises in Balti and Tandoori dishes, and there are gourmet evenings, which give customers an opportunity to try a wider variety of dishes.

An extensive range of Indian beers is available to enhance the Indian experience. Mr Ahmed and his brother who run the restaurant support many local charities giving a great deal of their time to help local people. We are very pleased that they have chosen to support this book by providing a scrumptious buffet menu.

Starters

The Vegetable Pakora

Ingredients

1lb (450g) flour
¾pint (475ml) water
1 teaspoon (to taste) salt
1 teaspoon (to taste) chilli powder
1 teaspoon whole coriander seeds
1 teaspoon whole cumin seeds
½lb (225g) vegetables (onion, cauliflower, potato)
Sufficient quantity cooking oil for deep frying

Preparing Vegetable Pakora :

First boil potatoes, then skin them whilst they are still warm. Now let them cool. Separate cauliflower into small bits and boil in salted water for 1½ minutes. Now drain in cold water. By now the potatoes should be cool enough to dice with the onion. Mix the flour, salt, chilli powder, coriander seeds and cumin seeds, gently pouring in the water whilst mixing. Leave the dough for ½ hour. Heat the oil to about 170°C/340°F. Take a tablespoon of the mixture and gently pour into the heated oil. Once it has browned evenly all over, remove from oil and leave it on the kitchen paper to drain. Repeat until all the mixture is used up.

Pakora Sauce

Ingredients

8 tablespoons tomato sauce
2 tablespoons onion (finely chopped)
2 tablespoons fresh tomatoes (finely chopped)
½ teaspoon chilli powder
½ teaspoon salt
Pinch sugar
1 green chilli (finely chopped) to taste
4 tablespoons water

Mix all ingredients and allow to stand for at least an hour before serving.

Spicy Balti Potatoes

Balti is a type of Kashmiri curry which originated in Baltistan in Northern Pakistan.

The indigenous peoples of Baltistan were nomads who ate meat from their own flock or hunted game. They used a Karahi to cook any available meat and vegetables with the addition of dried spices. The long slow cooking process, on a pile if glowing embers, resulted in a tender and fragrant 'casserole'; thus did Balti cooking originate.

It has been around in the UK, mostly in the Midlands for the last 20 years, but only recently has it gained widespread popularity. Balti cooking is epitomised by the subtle flavours of the ingredients often based on onions and tomatoes, with cumin, coriander and Fenugreek being the most popular spices.

Baltis are traditionally served with bread, instead of rice and are eaten without cutlery! Break off a small piece of bread and use it to scoop up a mouthful of Balti.

Ingredients

3 tablespoons corn oil
½ teaspoon white cumin seeds
3 curry leaves
1 teaspoon crushed dried red chillies
½ teaspoon mixed onion, mustard and fenugreek seeds
1 teaspoon fennel seeds
3 garlic cloves
½ teaspoon shredded ginger
2 medium onions, sliced
6 new potatoes cut into 5mm (¼") slices
1 tablespoon chopped fresh coriander
1 fresh red chilli, seeded and sliced
1 fresh green chilli seeded and sliced

Method

Heat the oil in a Karahi.* Lower the heat slightly and add the cumin seeds, curry leaves, dried red chillies, mixed onion, mustard and fenugreek seeds, fennel seeds, garlic cloves and ginger. Fry for about 1 minute and then add the onions and fry for 5 minutes or until the onions are golden brown. Add the potatoes, fresh coriander and fresh red and green chillies and mix well. Cover the pan tightly with foil, making sure the foil does not touch the food. Cook over a very low heat for about 7 minutes or until potatoes are tender. Remove the foil and serve hot. *See glossary

King Prawn Bhoona

Ingredients

1lb (450g) king prawns (peeled and washed)
4oz (125g) butter
4oz (125g) onion (chopped)
3 cloves garlic (crushed and chopped finely)
2 teaspoons ginger (crushed and chopped finely)
8oz (250g) tomatoes (peeled and chopped)
1 teaspoon fenugreek seeds
4 cloves
2 cardamom pods (black)
1" stick cinnamon
½ teaspoon turmeric
2 teaspoon chilli powder
1 ½ teaspoon salt
¼ pint (150ml) tamarind water
2 spring onion (chopped)

Method

Melt the butter, fry the onion, garlic, ginger, tomatoes, fenugreek seeds, cloves, cardamom and cinnamon until the onion is golden brown. Add the salt, turmeric and chilli powder and the prawns, and continue cooking until the prawns are firm and bright pink. Stir in the tamarind water, cover and simmer gently for about 10 minutes. Lastly stir in the chopped spring onions and cook for another 5 minutes with the lid off.

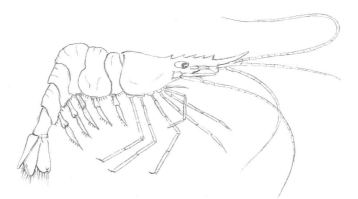

Lamb Korma

Ingredients

2lb (900g) leg or fillet of lamb, boned and diced
4oz (125g) sliced onion
3 cloves finely sliced garlic
2 teaspoons bruised and finely chopped fresh ginger
3 cardamom pods (black)
5 cloves
2" stick cinnamon
½ teaspoon turmeric
2 teaspoons ground cumin
2 teaspoons ground coriander
2 teaspoons red chilli powder
½ pint (300ml) water
4oz(125g) chopped finely tomatoes
1 ½ teaspoons salt
1 tablespoon garam masala
6oz (185g) coconut (creamed and desiccated)
5fl oz (150ml) yoghurt (plain)
2 tablespoons fresh coriander leaves (optional)

Method

Fry the onion, garlic and ginger, until the onion is soft. Add the spices, excluding the garam masala at this stage. Cook gently but thoroughly for about 20 minutes, stirring the pan occasionally to prevent sticking. Add the meat, increase the heat to moderate and continue to fry until the meat is well coloured. Pour in the water, cover, and simmer gently until the meat is tender (about 35 minutes). Now add the tomatoes, salt, garam masala and coconut and simmer until the sauce has almost evaporated, then add the yoghurt and coriander leaves (if used). Heat thoroughly and serve.

If you prefer a 'hotter sauce', try adding a few chopped green chillies at the end. On the other hand, if it is too hot, add some more yoghurt and a squeeze of lemon juice; even another tablespoon or two of coconut will tame it down a little. Indeed, the real secret of home-cooked curries lies in experimentation. Don't be frightened to leave out the garlic if your mother-in-law can't eat it. Your Korma will be different, but still delicious.

Balti Lahori Gosht

Lahore is in the North of Pakistan quite near the Indian Border. In the days of the great Mongol Emperors, Kagire was a major city connecting Agra and Delhi in the north. A great tree-lined road was especially built to facilitate the emperor's biannual procession between these cities, involving hundreds of elephants, thousands of camels and horses and tens of thousands of camp followers. Every night a new camp was built and the cooking began. This aromatic dish would have been one they enjoyed served with Pilau rice and chutney.

Ingredients

1lb of rump steak cut into 1" cubes
2-3 teaspoons ghee or corn oil
3-6 garlic cloves (finely chopped)

For the Spices :
1 teaspoon white cumin seeds
1 teaspoon sesame seeds
¼ teaspoon fennel seeds
¼ teaspoon aniseed
6-8 green cardamom seeds
4-6 cloves
2in (5cm) piece Cassia bark
¼ teaspoon turmeric
8oz (225g) onion (very finely chopped)
3-4 tablespoons Balti masala paste
About 7fl oz (200ml) reserved stock, chicken stock or water
8fl oz (200ml) thick double cream
2 teaspoons granulated sugar
1 tablespoon Balti garam masala
1 tablespoon very finely chopped fresh coriander leaves
*Aromatic salt to taste *See glossary*

Method

Heat the Ghee or oil in a Karahi on high heat, then stir-fry the garlic and spices for 30 seconds. Add the onion on a reduced heat and stir-fry for about 10 minutes, allowing the onion to become translucent and begin to brown. Add the masala paste and the meat. Raise the heat again and bring to a brisk sizzle, stir-frying as needed for 5 minutes. Add the reserved stock or water, bit by bit, and simmer, stirring on a lower heat for about 10 minutes. Add the cream and sugar and test for tenderness. If more cooking is needed add stock or water as required. When the flavour is correct, add the garam masala, fresh coriander leaves and aromatic, salt to taste. Simmer for 15 minutes more, then serve.

Vegetable Curry

Ingredients

4 tablespoons Ghee or butter
4oz (125g) onion
2 cloves garlic (crushed and finely chopped)
1oz (30g) ginger, bruised and finely chopped
4oz (125g) chopped tomatoes
1 teaspoon turmeric
1 ½ teaspoon chilli powder
Salt
6oz (185g) cauliflower
6oz (185g) peeled and diced potatoes
¾ pint (450ml) water
4oz (125g) peas
2 teaspoons garam masala

Method

Melt the ghee or butter and fry the onion, garlic and ginger until golden brown. Add the tomatoes, turmeric, chilli powder and salt and cook for 5 more minutes. Divide the cauliflower into florets and add them with the potatoes to the spice mixture in the pan. Coat them well, and then pour in the water. Cover and simmer gently for 10 minutes, then add the peas and cook for a further 8-10 minutes. Sprinkle the garam masala over, leave for 5 minutes before serving.

Indian Vegetable

Ingredients

5oz (156g) Bhindi (Lady fingers / Okra), trimmed and sliced
5oz (156g) aubergine (egg plant), peeled and sliced
3oz (94g) diced tinda (squash) *
5oz (156g) karela (bitter gourd) peeled and diced *
4oz (125g) onion
2 cloves garlic, crushed and finely chopped
2 teaspoons ginger grated or finely chopped
1 teaspoon turmeric
1 teaspoon chilli powder
1½ teaspoons salt
1-2 tablespoon garam masala
½ pint (300ml) water
4 tablespoon Ghee or cooking oil

Method

Keeping the aubergine and karela separate, sprinkle them both thickly with the cooking salt and leave for several hours if possible. Then drain away the water which will have collected and rinse them well. The karela will now need to be blanched in boiling water for two minutes. Melt the ghee and fry the onion, garlic, ginger with the turmeric, chilli powder and salt until the onion is well cooked and golden brown. Add all the vegetables and fry gently for 10 minutes or so. Add the water, cover and cook for a further 10 minutes until the vegetables are tender. Sprinkle the garam masala over. If the liquid is too thin, boil it away quickly for a minute.

Naan Bread

Ingredients

1 teaspoon caster (superfine) sugar
1 teaspoon dried yeast
150ml (¼ pint) warm water
225g (8oz) plain flour, plus extra for dusting
1 tsp ghee melted
1 tsp salt
50g (2oz) unsalted butter, melted
1 teaspoon poppy seeds

Method

Put the sugar and yeast into a small bowl and add the warm water. Mix well until the yeast has dissolved, and leave for about 10 minutes or until frothy. Place the flour in a large mixing bowl, make a well in the mixture, add melted ghee and yeast mixture. Mix well, using your hands, add a little more water if the dough is too dry. Turn the dough out on to a lightly floured surface and knead for about 5 minutes. Put the dough back into the bowl, cover and leave in a warm place for about 1½ hours, or until double in size. Turn out onto a floured surface and knead for 5 more minutes. Break off small pieces of dough and roll into rounds about 13cm (5 in) in diameter and 1cm (½in) thick. Place naans on greased foil under a very hot grill for about 7-10 minutes. Turn twice and brush with melted butter and sprinkle with poppy seeds. Serve immediately or keep wrapped in foil until required.

PITTODRIE HOUSE HOTEL

I have been brought up within sight of Bennachie, and have happy childhood memories of annual family pilgrimages to picnic and then climb the mountain, which is a notable Aberdeenshire landmark. I had no hesitation in telling a friend recently when asked how to get to Pittodrie House, that it was at the bottom of Bennachie. Not exactly the right answer, but one many North-East people familiar with the area may have given.

Pittodrie House stands in the shadow of Bennachie in 3,000 acres of gardens and parkland. It is a grand country house, steeped in history going as far back as Robert the Bruce, who granted the estate to the Earl of Mar for his loyalty at Bannockburn.

Outdoor pursuits are high on the list of activities for visitors with shooting, clay pigeons, fly fishing, four-by-four driving, off-road grass carting and hill walking to name but a few. I have enjoyed cuisine prepared under the eagle-eye of head chef Bob Ovington on several occasions. He makes especially good use of local ingredients: and Pittodrie has its own vegetable and herb garden. It is a gratifying experience to be served their own crisp green vegetables fresh from the garden.

This hotel is well known for Scottish country dances at New Year (Hogmonay). In the ballroom they roll back the carpet for the more formal dancing, and for those who want a more casual 'knees-up' the Ceilidh evening is a lot of fun.

A Wholemeal Crêpe filled with Woodland Mushrooms glazed with Garlic Breadcrumbs and Gruyère Cheese

Ingredients

For the Wholemeal Crêpe :
2oz wholemeal flour
2oz plain white flour
½ pint of milk
½ teaspoon of salt
2 tablespoons of olive oil
1 whole egg and egg yolk
Teaspoonful of chopped fresh parsley

For the Filling :
4oz Shiitake mushroom
4oz Chanterelles
4oz Ceps
4oz Chestnut mushrooms
2 large shallots
¼ pint double cream
1 pinch of nutmeg
1oz butter
2oz Gruyère cheese (grated)

For the Garlic Breadcrumbs :
2oz fresh breadcrumbs
2 cloves garlic (crushed)
½oz butter

Method

For the crêpes combine all ingredients together to form a batter and leave to stand. Make up 4 x 7" diameter thin crêpes. Leave to cool.

For the filling, dice up shallots finely and sweat off in butter. Add the mixed fungi sliced up, cook for 5 minutes. Add double cream and nutmeg. Put a spoonful of mixture into each crêpe and fold up. Fry 2oz of fresh breadcrumbs in butter slowly with the crushed garlic, until golden brown, place on top of each crêpe with a sprinkling of Gruyère cheese. Bake for about 5 minutes in a medium oven. Give two crêpes per person. Serve with a mixed leaf lettuce and vinaigrette dressing. (Serves 4)

Chef's Tip : The crêpe batter will make up to 10 x 7" pancakes which can be used as a starter or main course, depending on the size of the crepe pan used for cooking.

Supreme of Chicken Stuffed with Haggis Wrapped in Smoked Bacon with a Malt Whisky and Shallot Sauce

Ingredients

4 x 7oz skinned supremes fillets of chicken
8oz haggis
4 rashers of smoked bacon
4 large shallots finely diced
1oz flour
¾ pint chicken stock
5ml good malt whisky
2oz double cream
Salt and pepper
Sprigs of fresh tarragon to decorate

Method

Take supremes and make a pocket with a sharp knife. Put 2oz of haggis in the pocket, then wrap each supreme with smoked bacon.

Sauté the finely diced shallots in the flour, blending in the chicken stock and the whisky. Add the double cream, salt and pepper.

Bake supremes in a hot oven for about 20 minutes take out and leave to stand for 5 minutes to rest. Slice supremes, serve on 4 warmed plates with the malt whisky sauce poured round. Decorate with sprigs of tarragon. Serve with boiled new potatoes and stir fried vegetables. (Serves 4)

Dessert

Ginger and Vanilla Creme Brulée

Ingredients

¾ pint of double cream
6 egg yolks
4oz of crystallised stem ginger
½ teaspoon good vanilla flavouring or
1 fresh vanilla pod
1 tablespoon of caster sugar
2 tablespoons demerara sugar

Method

Take four (3 ½") ramekin dishes and place diced ginger into each one. In a bowl mix egg yolks, sugar and vanilla.

Bring cream to near boiling point and add egg yolk to mixture. In a clean pan stir mixture carefully over a medium heat until it starts to thicken. When it does, strain into a cold stainless steel bowl. Pour into ramekins and leave to cool.

When ready to serve, sprinkle each dish with demerara sugar and place under a hot grill until golden brown. Serve with langue de chat biscuits or shortbread. (Serves 4)

Chef's Tip : Be careful not to overcook egg mixture, otherwise you will end up with scrambled eggs.

Q BRASSERIE

The Q Brasserie is a first-floor restaurant in a former College of Divinity in the heart of Aberdeen. They have a new head chef called Jonathan Brown, whose genuine enthusiasm persuaded David McCallum - sous chef, Natacha Segar - pastry chef and Kevin Shand - chef tourer, to come in on their day off and prepare food for our photographs. This was greatly appreciated by the photographers and myself, and the results you can see are stunning.

I also received some wonderful tips on bread making from Natacha Segar and some much needed guidance on how to make tuilles from David McCallum. The bread was so good, that Berry, the photographer took it all home in his camera bag, I wasn't even offered a bite!

Amuse Bouche

Risotto de Trumpet de Mort with Truffle Oil

Ingredients

5oz butter
½pt vegetable stock
4oz risotto rice
2oz tarragon chopped
2 shallots finely diced
1 clove garlic crushed
4oz Trumpet de mort (or the mushroom of your choice)
1fl oz truffle oil
Lemon juice
¼pt double cream

Method

1.   In a heavy pan, melt the butter add the garlic and shallots, and sweat until pale and soft.

2.   Add rice, when the rice has made a sharp cracking noise in the pan add the stock and trumpets.

3.   Cook 5-10 minutes. Stirring regularly, the rice should be cooked through but still have some bite to it.

4.   Add the cream and tarragon.

5.   Combine the truffle oil and lemon juice.

6.   In small teacups place a tablespoon of risotto, sprinkle with truffle oil, mix and serve with homemade bread. (Serves 4)

Walnut and Raisin Bread

Ingredients

2 kg strong bread flour
1,200ml water
50g yeast
100g butter
Pinch salt
½ cup sugar
Cupful of walnuts
Cupful of raisins

Method

1. Add yeast to tepid water with half a cupful of sugar, stir until sugar is dissolved.

2. Sift flour into mixing bowl.

3. Add softened butter to flour and mix.

4. Add yeast mixture to flour and mix.

5. Knead well, prove until mixture doubles in size.

6. Knock back and portion into 4 sizes, knead in walnuts and raisins.

7. Prove for another 10-15 minutes.

8. Bake in a pre-heated oven at 180°C/350°F/gas mark 4 for 20-25 minutes.

Garlic and Herb Bread : Exactly the same as for walnut and raisin substituting- 100g of garlic oil instead of 100g butter, and ½ cupful of mixed herbs e.g dill, basil, chives etc. instead of raisins and walnuts.

Starter

Rosette of Seared Scallops with a Chervil Butter

Ingredients

12 scallops (large, trimmed and dried)
¼pt white wine vinegar
¼pt dry white wine
1 bunch chervil (chopped finely)
2 shallots (chopped finely)
1 bunch chives (chopped finely)
4 tomatoes (blanched, skinned, de-seeded and cut into small dice)
Salt and pepper
¼pt olive oil
2 lemons (squeezed)
¼pt double cream
½lb butter (cubed)
2 star anise
Serve with Parmesan tuilles (see following page)

Method

1.   Season the scallops and marinade in half the oil and lemon juice.

2.   In a heavy-based pan reduce the vinegar, white wine and shallots until almost dry, add the cream and bring to the boil.

3.   Take the pan off the heat, and carefully whisk in the butter cubes. This will thicken the sauce, and give a smooth finish to the end result.

4.   Add the chervil and tomato and season.

5.   In a dry frying pan over a very high heat add the scallops and flash fry for no more than 20 seconds on each side.

6.   On 4 plates arrange the scallops, salad leaves and sauce, sprinkle with chives and serve with Parmesan tuilles. (Serves 4)

Parmesan Tuilles

Ingredients

1 cup plain flour
1 cup freshly grated Parmesan
4 whole egg whites
2 tablsp butter

Method

1. Sieve flour into bowl.

2. Add all other ingredients.

3. Beat to a smooth paste (rest for 1 hour).

4. Place template on a baking sheet, spread mixture over, remove template. Bake at 180°C/350°F/gas mark 4 for 3-4 minutes, until light golden brown.

Chef's Tip : Chill baking tray smeared with butter (in freezer). Spread tuille mixture onto baking sheet, which will hold the tuille in place.

For sweet tuilles, replace 1 cup Parmesan cheese with 1 cup of icing sugar and add cinnamon or vanilla seeds. (Serves 4)

Fillet of Beef with Herbs, Roasted Shallots and a Tarragon Cream Sauce

Ingredients

4 x 6oz beef fillets
20 shallots peeled
4oz butter
2oz sugar
1 pinch of dried tarragon

½pt of chicken or veal stock
½pt double cream
1 bunch chopped tarragon
1 tsp Dijon mustard
Salt and pepper

Method

1. Pre-heat the oven to 240°C/475°F/gas mark 9.

2. Melt 2oz butter, add shallots, coat well, sprinkle over sugar. Cook over a high heat until shallots can be pierced by a knife and are brown in colour.

3. In a heavy-based frying pan melt half of the butter over a high heat.

4. When the butter is foaming, add the seasoned fillets.

5. Sear all over until golden brown and place in the oven.

6. Cook to your preference - rare is about 15 minutes, well done about 25 minutes.

7. Remove fillets from the oven, rest in a warm place.

8. Add the mustard to the juices left in the pan and cook for one minute over a low heat.

9. Add the stock and reduce by half.

10. Add the cream and tarragon and bring to the boil.

11. Remove the whole shallots from the cooking juices, and fry until light brown.

12. Re-heat the fillets for about 3 minutes, arrange on 4 serving plates, arrange the shallots and pour over the sauce. Serve. (Serves 4)

Dessert

Sablé of Pear and Chocolate Sabayon

Ingredients

For the Sablé Biscuits :
1 egg
2oz sugar
5oz butter
8oz flour
Salt

For the Chocolate Sabayon :
3 egg yolks
2oz plain chocolate
¼pt white wine
¼lb sugar

For the Pears :
8 ripe pears peeled cored and halved
½lb sugar
½pt water
1 lemon (zest removed and squeezed)
1 cinnamon stick
1 clove
2 peppercorns

For the Crème Chantilly :
½pt double cream
2oz icing sugar

Method

1.   For the Sablé Biscuits: Rub in butter to flour, add sugar and a pinch of salt until it resembles breadcrumbs. Add egg to bind. Form into a ball. Roll out and cut into 12 circles of 3½" each. Bake pastry at 180°C/350°F/gas mark 4, until just brown. Leave to cool.

2.   For the Pears: Combine xsugar and water. Boil together for 10 minutes. Add the pears to the cooked syrup with the rest of the ingredients and poach gently for 6-7 minutes.

3.   For Chocolate Sabayon: Over a pan of boiling water whisk the sugar, white wine and egg yolks, in a bowl until very pale, fluffy and thick. Fold in the melted chocolate.

4.   For the Crème Chantilly: Whip the double cream until it is holding its shape, fold in the sugar.

To Serve

Place a small teaspoon of cream on the plate to allow the sablé biscuits to stick to the plate. Slice a pear and place a layer on the biscuit. Add a spoonful of chocolate sabayon, and then another spoonful of creme, pat on top of chocolate sabayon. Place another biscuit on top slightly skew, and do the same as above. (Serves 4)

THE ROYAL THAI

This most successful Aberdeen restaurant is run efficiently and to a very high standard by Simon Wang. Head chef Peter Tang has provided us with a typical buffet menu served at the restaurant.

To introduce Thai cookery in our book I have enlisted the help of Ladawaan Anderson from Thailand, who owns the Monaltrie Hotel in Ballater. Her popular Thai cookery courses are well known locally as is the cuisine at her hotel. She has written a most informative introduction to our Thai buffet from The Royal Thai, which I know you will enjoy!

Thai cooks have never been in the habit of recording measurements of ingredients or time of cooking. They cook by experience and 'feel' and the art is handed down in families, and among friends, by practice.

The Thai make much use in their food of such condiments, seasonings, sauces and flavourings as fish sauce (Nam Pla), shrimp paste (Ka Pi), curry powders, soy sauce, coconut milk and cream, tamarind, limes and many kinds of spices, including cardamom, coriander, anise and other seeds as well as cloves, nutmeg, ginger and cinnamon.

These highly-seasoned dishes are locally called 'with the rice' dishes because rice is the main dish, being to the Thais what bread is to the European. For centuries, the Thai have naturally enriched their polished rice by serving it with many sauces and condiments, some of which are exceedingly rich in vitamin K, soy sauce contains B group vitamins and the various sweet and hot peppers, tamarinds and limes are rich in vitamin C. Shrimp paste is almost all protein.

A proper Thai meal consists of steamed rice served with Gaeng Chued (a clear soup), a steamed dish, a fried dish, a Yam (salad), and a Kreung jim, a very strong hot sauce, and finally fruit.

Ladawaan Anderson

Starters

Chicken Royal Parcel

Ingredients

Pandon leaves
12oz marinated chicken fillet
2tsp fish sauce
1tsp sugar
1tsp salt
1oz sesame seeds

Method

Marinade the chicken for two hours in the fish sauce, sugar, salt and sesame seeds. Wrap with the pandan leaves (secure with cocktail stick) then fry well. Accompany with chilli chicken sauce. The chicken should only be removed from the leaf, just prior to eating.

Thai Fish Cakes

Ingredients

2lb of fresh boneless monkfish tail
2oz of red chilli paste
1oz of crushed lemon leaves
2oz of crushed long beans
1oz of coriander
1oz of lemon grass
2oz of fish sauce
2tsp sugar

Method

Use a food mixer to turn the ingredients into a fine smooth paste. Roll 2 level tablespoons of mixture into a ball, flatten slightly; repeat with remaining mixture. Just before serving deep-fry fish cakes in hot oil until well browned and cooked; drain on absorbent paper.

Tiger in Tears Cold Beef Salad

Ingredients

2lb of grilled top grade sirloin steak, cooled and cut into strips
1tsp of lemon grass
1tsp of mint
2tsp of coriander
1tsp of crushed dried chilli
3oz crushed onion
3tsp of fish sauce
3tsp of sugar
4tsp of fresh lime juice
4tsp of crushed roasted rice
Thinly sliced cucumber and tomato

Method

Mix all ingredients with the thinly sliced sirloin, serve on a bed of lettuce.

Main Courses

Homok Talay

Ingredients

2lb of fresh seafood (squid/ king prawns/ mussels/ crab claws/ monkfish)
1oz curry paste
1tsp lemon leaves
2tsp chilli
1oz green pepper
1oz red pepper
3tsp fish sauce
3tsp sugar
1tsp lemon grass
5oz coconut milk
5fl oz of top quality stock

Method

Heat oil, add curry paste and stir for a few seconds, add other ingredients except fish sauce and sugar. Bring to the boil, stirring well. Add seafood and cook through gently, finally stir in sugar and fish sauce.

Beef Emperor

Ingredients

2lb top quality topside, sliced thinly
oil
1 tablsp flour
1tsp garlic
1oz spring onion
1oz mushroom
3tsp oyster sauce
2tsp sugar
2tsp fish sauce
5fl oz of top quality consommé

Method

Mix garlic, spring onion, sugar and flour with beef and marinade for 1 hour. Fry beef in oil, add consommé and mushroom, cook for 2 minutes. Finally, fold in oyster sauce and fish sauce. Serve with rice.

Chuchi Prawns

Ingredients

2lb top quality peeled super king prawns
2oz red curry paste
1tsp lime leaves
1tsp tamarind
2tsp chilli
2tsp coriander
1oz green pepper
1oz red pepper
3tsp fish sauce
3tsp sugar
5oz coconut milk
5fl oz of top quality stock

Method

Heat oil, add curry paste and stir for a few seconds, add other ingredients except fish sauce and sugar. Bring to the boil, stirring well. Add prawns and cook through gently, finally stir in sugar and fish sauce.

Noodles Siam

Ingredients

½ lb Thai noodles
2 eggs beaten
½ lb barbecued pork or other meat
Shrimps
Assorted vegetable e.g ½ small cabbage, 2 small carrots, garlic
Spring onion
1 tablsp curry powder
1 tsp chilli powder
1 tablsp fish sauce
1 tsp sugar
Coriander to garnish

Method

Soak the Thai noodles overnight. Heat the oil adding the garlic and meat, stirring until cooked. Add beaten egg then vegetables, spring onion, fish sauce, sugar, curry and chilli powder. Add the shrimps and noodles, stir until heated through, serve sprinkled with coriander.

THE SILVER DARLING

At the end of Pocra Quay, near 'Fittie' (Footdee) in Old Aberdeen, The Silver Darling Restaurant witnesses all traffic leaving and entering Aberdeen harbour. It is a fascinating location for a restaurant, recognised by Didier Dejean, owner of The Silver Darling, who has just completely refurbished his brand new rooftop restaurant. From every seat in the restaurant you have the opportunity, to see in one direction the working marine traffic of an oil based city, and in the other, miles of sandy beach stretching as far as Cruden Bay.

Didier is justifiably delighted with the new restaurant and kitchen, gleaming and magnificent. The accent is French and not surprisingly, seafood is the speciality. Food is imaginative and sometimes elaborate, and we hope the photographs do the menu credit. With Didier's energetic enthusiasm, this new restaurant can only be a success.

Starter

Gite de Thon Frais en Carpaccio Au Pistou

Ingredients

250g of fresh tuna (loin)
1 bouquet of fresh basil (chopped)
2 soup-spoons of olive oil
1 clove of garlic (chopped)
Salt and pepper

Method

1. Cut the fillet of tuna into wafer-thin escalopes (slices).

2. Mix chopped basil, olive oil, garlic, salt and pepper into a fine green paste.

3. Lay raw escalopes of tuna on a cold plate (see picture).

4. With a brush, spread the tuna with the green paste.

5. Serve cold with a green salad and walnut oil dressing. (Serves 4)

Main Course

La Bourride

'One of the greatest dishes of Provence'

Ingredients

2 live lobsters
4 fillets of thick white fish (bass, monkfish, turbot, red snapper)
7fl oz (200ml) double cream
½ pint (300ml) aïoli (mayonnaise with a lot of garlic)

For the Stock:
2 pints of water
200ml white wine
Fish heads x 2
1 leek chopped
1 fennel chopped
1 onion chopped
1 bayleaf

Method

1. Simmer the stock for 25 minutes and strain.

2. Into the strained stock place the lobsters, and bring to the boil, reduce heat and simmer for 20 minutes.

3. Remove lobsters and keep warm while you poach the white fish fillets - keep these warm also.

4. Now reduce the remaining stock to a third, and over a low heat stir the cream. Carefully whisk half of the aïoli into the sauce until the sauce takes on the colour and consistency of custard. Pour over the fish and serve at once.

5. You can serve with crispy croutons and boiled new potatoes. (Serves 4)

Dessert

Gratin a l'Orange

Ingredients

6 egg yolks
6 egg whites
80g caster sugar
50g plain flour
180ml double cream
150ml orange juice or coulis
3 gelatine leaves (in cold water)
Icing sugar for decoration

Method

1.   Boil double cream and orange juice or coulis.

2.   Into a bowl mix yolks, sugar and flour together to form a paste.

3.   Add boiling cream to the paste.

4.   Put back to heat and stir non stop until just at the boiling point, transfer immediately to a large bowl (to stop it cooking).

5.   Add the soft gelatine and stir until setting point is reached.

6.   Whisk the whites and add gently to the pastry cream.

7.   Prepare 4 rings 3" wide by 1 inch deep, fill them right up to the top using a spatula and reserve for 1 hour in the fridge.

8.   Take ring out from fridge. Remove the mousse and top with icing sugar, place under a hot grill until golden brown.

9.   Serve immediately with a raspberry coulis. (Serves 4)

SIMPSON'S HOTEL, RESTAURANT & BRASSERIE

Simpson's Hotel, Restaurant and Brasserie, situated in the West End of Aberdeen opened this year to great acclaim. This small luxury hotel has been painstakingly designed and decorated with the warm welcoming colours of the Riviera.

The hotel has been described as a "pearl in the sea of granite" because of the high standards in design, décor and food, which the Simpson family are known to provide. Head chef Paul Whitecross very kindly provided us with a menu befitting the stunning Brasserie where Moroccan columns reach up on both sides to support a colonnade of arches. At the foot of the sweeping staircase a fountain pours water in front of palms and exotic flowers.

Paul has created a most dazzlingly varied menu for the Brasserie which enhances that sunny Mediterranean feeling created by the décor. He has won numerous awards for his most creative cookery.

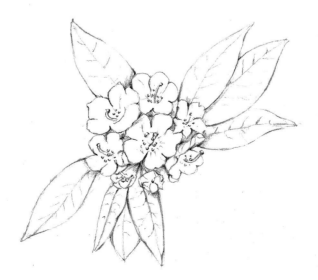

Vichyssoise of Cod Viennoise

Ingredients

500g leeks white only, finely sliced
200g potatoes, peeled and finely chopped
125g onions, peeled, finely sliced
Garlic peeled and sliced
30fl oz fish stock brought to the boil
30fl oz double cream
50g unsalted butter
Freshly ground white pepper and salt to taste

For the Garnish :
4 x 125g pieces of cod

For the Viennoise :
1 ½oz equal quantities basil and parsley
50g Parmesan cheese - grated
75g fresh breadcrumbs
50g unsalted butter, softened
Freshly ground white pepper and salt

For the Crushed Potatoes :
375g new potatoes, skinned and washed
50g leeks - sliced thinly, washed and blanched
Juice of ½ lemon

Method

1.   To make viennoise place all the ingredients into a food processor and process until throughly mixed. Keep stopping and stir around the processed ingredients with a spatula to make sure that none of the mixture is stuck under the blade. Then spread the mixture onto greaseproof paper, place another piece on top and roll out evenly to your required thickness and freeze. When frozen take out and cut into quantities to the size of the cod pieces.

2.	For the crushed new potatoes, firstly boil for about 15 minutes or until just tender. Then drain and return to a warm stove, add the olive oil and crush with a fork. Then add the leeks, juice of half a lemon and the basil, and adjust the seasoning remembering to keep the mixture warm.

3.	To make the soup, sweat off the onions, garlic, leeks and potatoes in butter. In a large pan without colouring, cover with the fish stock and cook for about 10 minutes. Add the cream and cook for a further three or four minutes and place in a food processor and purée. Then pass through a fine sieve and season to taste.

4.	For the presentation, place mixture in the centre of 4 hot soup bowls using pastry cutter, place the potato mixture into the centre and top with the cod and a slice of viennoise then glaze with a blow torch until golden. Pour the soup around and serve. (Serves 4)

Prime Fillet of Scottish Beef, Turnip Dauphinoise and Wild Mushrooms

Ingredients

5 x 225g beef fillet
20 sprigs of chervil
Non-scented oil

For the Sauce :
9fl oz red wine
10fl oz veal stock
1 sprig thyme
1 bay leaf
2 shallots peeled and diced
1 garlic clove peeled and diced
Salt and pepper to taste

For the Turnip Dauhinoise :
1.25kg turnip peeled, sliced very thin
2 cloves of garlic, crushed
24fl oz double cream
100g mature cheddar cheese, grated

For the Garnish :
12 peeled shallots, cooked al dente and caramelised with a little sugar
6oz mixed wild mushrooms
12 baby carrots, washed and cooked with a slight bite (al dente)
2 tablsp butter

Method

The first step is to prepare the turnip Dauphinoise. Start by buttering an ovenproof dish. Bring to the boil the cream and garlic and layer this in the dish with the turnip alternately. Cover with enough of the cream mixture and sprinkle on the cheese. Bake in a preheated oven for about 45 minutes.

Remove and place a heavy weight on top and allow to cool. When cold cut into required shape or size. I usually cut them into a disc. Reheat when required.

The next step is to cook the fillets. Season them on both sides and put the non-scented oil in a frying pan. When hot, cook the meat on all sides until evenly golden, place in a hot oven and cook to your preference.

In a sauté pan, heat a little butter until it starts to foam, quickly sauté the wild mushrooms until cooked and season. Reheat the carrots by sautéing in a little butter, and season. Reheat the shallots in the oven until warm through.

To make the sauce, add the shallots and garlic to the beef pan. Deglaze with red wine reducing until nearly evaporated. Add the stock, thyme and bayleaf and reduce by half. Pass through a fine sieve, and adjust the seasoning.

To serve place the turnip Dauphinoise in the centre of the plates, top with the fillets of beef, arrange alternately around the mushroom, shallots and carrots. Pour the sauce around, not over the meat, garnish with 4 sprigs of thyme on each plate and serve. (Serves 5)

Dessert

Drambuie Flavoured Tiramisu and Coffee Bean Ice-Cream

Ingredients

For the Tiramisu :
250g Marscarpone cheese
250g double cream, lightly whipped to a ribbon stoge
3 egg yolks
100g caster sugar
2½ gelatine leaves soaked
Drambuie to taste
8 sponge discs soaked in Drambuie

For the Coffee Bean Ice-Cream :
10fl oz double cream
10fl oz milk
1 vanilla pod
12 coffee beans
190g egg yolks
190g caster sugar
190g good quality Couverture chocolate

For the Tuille Biscuit :
100g unsalted butter
200g plain flour
200g icing sugar
2 egg whites

Method

1. To make the tiramisu, whisk the egg yolks and sugar in a bowl over a warm saucepan. To make a sabayon, remove from heat and add the soaked gelatine leaves. Fold in the marscapone, followed by the Drambuie and cream. In a small gateau mould, place a sponge disc at the bottom and top with the tiramisu and leave in the refrigerator to set.

2. Prepare the ice-cream, by bringing to the boil the milk and cream with the coffee beans and vanilla pod split into two. Beat the egg yolks and sugar until pale and light (this can be done with a mixer). Pour on the cream, stirring and return to the stove to cook out - i.e until the mixture coats the back of the spoon. Sieve and add the chocolate. Allow to cool and place into an ice-cream machine until

thickened. If you don't have a machine, simply place the mixture onto a freezer tray or bowl and freeze stirring regularly until set.

3. For the tuille biscuit, combine the icing sugar and butter, beat until light and creamy, add the egg whites, a little at a time, then fold in the flour. (At Simpson's they make stencils to make a sailing ship, mast and oars). Bake at 180°C/350°F or gas mark 4 until lightly brown around the edges.

4. Finally the presentation: assemble the sailing ship and place onto the plate towards one half. I usually fan a little chocolate sauce and sauce anglaise (custard) on the other half of the plate. Unmould the tiramisu, gently placing it on the plate, opposite. Top with a scoop of the ice-cream and a sprig of mint. (Serves 8)

THAINSTONE HOUSE HOTEL
AND COUNTRY CLUB

Thainstone House Hotel and Country Club has a long history of excellent food under head chef Alan Donald, who came to the area from Gleneagles. Alan has laid down a foundation of good local supplies: beef from Inverurie and salmon from Deeside. These together with seafood all feature heavily on the menu. The hotel's restaurant is well known for fine food and has been awarded two AA stars.

This four star hotel is picturesquely situated in the heart of the castle and whisky trail but caters for locals as well as tourists. Its attractive surroundings make it a popular venue for summer weddings.

Panache of North-East Seafood in a Saffron Nage with Strips of Seasonal Vegetables

Ingredients

1lb seabass filleted, scaled and pin boned
4 fresh scallops with roe attached
4 fresh langoustine tails shelled
1 fresh monkfish tail cleaned of all membrane
1 litre fish consommé infused with saffron
80g julienne of carrot
80g julienne of leek
80g julienne of courgette
40g chopped fresh coriander
Salt and freshly ground white pepper

Method

Divide and cut fish and shellfish evenly between 4 portions. Heat the fish consommé infused with saffron and poach the seafood over a low heat until cooked. Remove seafood from consommé and put on a tray to rest. Add the vegetable juliennes to the consommé and cook till 'al dente'.

To Serve

Divide the seafood equally between 4 medium-sized bowls. Drain the vegetable julienne and place an even spiral on top of the seafood. Add the chopped fresh coriander to the fish consommé and pour Nage over the seafood. Serve immediately. (Serves 4)

Roast Breast of Pheasant, Confit of Leg, with Spinach, Shiitake Mushrooms, Fondant Potatoes & Sherry Vinegar Infused Jus

Ingredients

2 oven ready pheasants remove the legs and confit in goose fat
400g picked and washed spinach
120g sliced Shiitake mushrooms
5ml lemon juice
40g finely chopped shallots
Freshly grated nutmeg to taste
½pt game jus (stock)
2 tablsp sherry vinegar
12 fondant potatoes
250g unsalted butter
1pt chicken stock
100g courgettes diced
Salt and freshly ground black pepper
Olive oil

Method

Season the pheasant crowns and roast in a hot oven until cooked. Remove from the oven and leave to rest. Roast pheasant legs in goose fat, in a small pan with a lid until the meat is falling from the bone. Deglaze the pan with sherry vinegar, add the game jus, simmer and season. Sweat the shallots and Shiitake mushrooms in 25g og butter, add the spinach. Season with salt and pepper and freshly ground nutmeg. For the fondant potatoes take a flat-based pan and line it with 175g of sliced butter. Cut potatoes into squares of about 7cm wide and 4cm deep. Place these flat down onto the butter. Add the chicken stock to the pan. Place on the heat and cook until the liquid has reduced and the butter has been absorbed into the potatoes. Then roast the courgettes in hot olive oil and add a little lemon juice to taste. Remove confit of leg from bone, tear into strips and keep warm.

To Serve

Remove pheasant breasts from bone and slice. Place a tower of spinach and mushroom in the middle of each plate, top with confit then sliced breast meat. Place 3 fondant potatoes around each plate, scatter roasted courgettes around. Finish the game jus sauce by adding the 50g of cubed butter, allowing each cube of butter to melt before the next addition, this will thicken the sauce. Pour around plate and serve immediately. (Serves 4)

Dessert

Rich Chocolate Cake with Heather Honey and Glenmorangie Ice-Cream

Ingredients

For the Cake :
225g (8oz) good quality plain chocolate
225g (8oz) unsalted butter
150g (5oz) caster sugar
6 medium egg yolks
8 medium egg whites
Sifted icing sugar to garnish

Method

Pre-heat the oven to 170°C/325°F/gas mark 3. Lightly butter a 25cm (10inch) springform cake tin and then line the base with a circle of silicone paper.

Break the chocolate into a bowl and add the butter. Rest mixture over a pan of simmering water, making sure that the bowl does not touch the water. Leave to melt, stirring until it is smooth. Remove - set aside. Put the sugar and egg yolks into a large bowl and whisk together until the mixture becomes pale and thick. Gently fold this into the melted chocolate.

Now whisk the egg whites into soft peaks. Very gently fold the whites into the chocolate mixture. Pour into the tin and bake for 45 minutes. It will soufflé up and just crack when ready. Leave to cool in the tin until ready to serve with the Ice-Cream. (Serves 4-6)

Heather Honey & Glenmorangie Ice-Cream

Ingredients

600ml (1 pint) milk
6 medium egg yolks
25g (1oz) caster sugar
150g (5oz) heather honey
50ml (2fl oz) Glenmorangie malt whisky
85ml (3fl oz) double cream

Method

Pour the milk into a pan and bring to the boil. Meanwhile, whisk the egg yolks and sugar together in a bowl till pale and creamy. Whisk in the hot milk, return the mixture to the pan and cook over a gentle heat, stirring constantly until it thickens enough to coat the back of the wooden spoon lightly. Pour the mixture into a bowl and stir in the honey, whisky and double cream. Leave until cold and then cover and place in the fridge until well chilled.

Then either churn the mixture in an ice-cream maker or pour it into a shallow plastic bowl and freeze until almost firm. Scrape the mixture into a food processor and whizz until smooth. Pour it back into the bowl and repeat once more. Return the ice-cream to the freezer and freeze until firm.

For the best results remove the ice-cream from the freezer about 10 minutes before serving to soften slightly . (Serves 4-6)

THE TOLBOOTH

Stonehaven is a picturesque town on the coast just South of Aberdeen. The harbour still supports a fishing fleet. The Tolbooth is one of Stonehaven's oldest buildings overlooking the harbour, standing ten feet from the North Sea. Of course they specialise in seafood, what else could they do at such a location? Local fish are landed at Stonehaven harbour on a regular basis and more exotic fish miraculously find their way into the kitchen.

The proprietors are Chris McCarrey and Jean-François Medar, Jean is also head chef. He is half French, half Dutch and has an Australian assistant chef. Between them they are creating imaginative, tantalising menus, most sought after in the area. Examples are Roasted Red Pepper Soup with a Zhoug Relish (from the Yemen) and Mussels in Coconut Sauce with strong Thai overtones. These wonderful dishes they have kindly given us for the cookbook.

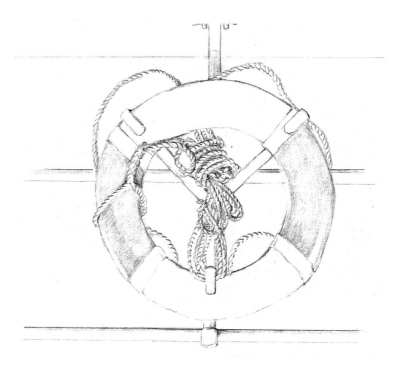

BUFFET MENU

Starters

Roasted Red Pepper Soup with Zhoug relish

Ingredients

2lbs red peppers
3 carrots
1 large onion
6 fresh tomatoes
1 teaspoon of paprika
½ teaspoon cayenne pepper
6 tablespoons rice
3 pints vegetable stock
Salt and pepper

For the Zhoug Relish :
1 small bunch of coriander
2 cloves of garlic
1 deseeded green chilli
2 tablespoons ground cumin
2 tablespoons olive oil

Method

Roast the sliced, deseeded peppers, sliced onion, sliced carrot and whole tomatoes in a hot oven for 20-25 minutes. Place all of the vegetables in a pot with the stock, the rice, cayenne pepper and paprika and bring to the boil. Simmer for about 30 minutes. Blend the soup and pass it through a strainer. Season with salt and pepper

For the Zhoug relish, place all the above ingredients in a blender. Add salt and pepper. To serve place a spoonful in the middle of each bowl of soup. (Serves 6)

Port and Stilton Cheesecake

Ingredients

18 digestive biscuits
6 oatcakes
4 ½oz butter (melted)
3oz Stilton cheese
3oz caster sugar
3fl oz double cream
1lb Philadelphia cream cheese
1 teaspoon powdered gelatine
4fl oz port
2fl oz water

Method

Dissolve the gelatine in the water and add the port. Reduce over a medium heat to half the original volume. Put to one side to cool.

Mix the digestive biscuits and oatcakes with the butter in a blender and line the bottom of a cake tin (one with a removable base) with the mixture. Mix the double cream, sugar and cream cheese in a food processor. Crumble the stilton and add to the mixture. Place the cheese mixture on top of the biscuit base. Make a few fissures with a knife in the smoothed out cheese mixture and pour in port. Chill. (Serves 6-8)

Mussels in a Coconut Sauce

Ingredients

4lb mussels
2 chillies
1 blade lemon grass
2 peppers
1oz ginger
1 tin (400mls) coconut cream
1oz arrowroot
A little cream
2fl oz white wine

Method

Steam the mussels in a big pan with a little white wine, shake the pan so that all the mussels are open. Chop the chillies, lemon grass, peppers and ginger very finely, put in a pan and cook very briefly. Add the coconut milk and give a good stir. Thicken with arrowroot and add the cream. Check the seasoning.

Place half the mussel shells on a plate, pour over the sauce and garnish with some fresh herbs. Serve at once. (Serves 2)

Halibut Fillet with a Smoked Salmon Mousse

Ingredients

1 whole halibut
½lb smoked salmon scraps
2 whole eggs
2 tablsp Noilly Prat vermouth
A little white pepper
4fl oz whipping cream

Method

For the Halibut:
To fillet the halibut lay it flat in front of you and make a straight cut over the middle of it's back from head to tail. Now by placing your knife at an angle you can easily remove both fillets. Turn the fish round and repeat. Take the skin off and set the fillets aside.

For the Mousse:
Put the salmon scraps in to the blender (fast speed), add the Noilly Prat, eggs and white pepper. Pour the cream in very slowly. When it has reached a mousse like consistency take out of the blender and chill for 1 hour.

To complete the dish:
Make a neat cut sideways in the Halibut. Put the smoked salmon mousse in a piping bag and pipe a line in the fillet. Steam or poach for about 3 minutes. Drain and serve at once with a dill butter sauce. (Serves 2)

Dessert

Frozen Mocha Mousse

Ingredients

6 eggs
¼ pint double or whipping cream
2oz white chocolate
2oz milk chocolate
2oz dark, bitter chocolate
2 tablsp strong black coffee
3 tablsp liqueur (Cointreau, Tia Maria, Amaretto etc.)
3 tablsp caster sugar

Method

Separate the eggs and whisk the whites until stiff peaks form. Melt the white chocolate in a double boiler. Whisk ¼ pint double cream with 1 spoonful of caster sugar until soft peaks form. Add 2 egg yolks and whisk for another minute.

Add 1 spoonful of liqueur to the cream and egg yolks then add the melted chocolate. Whisk this mixture until firm and fold in the egg whites. Place the mixture in the bottom of a 2lb loaf tin and place in the freezer for 30 minutes.

Make the other two layers, repeating the process using the milk chocolate. When making the dark chocolate layer, add the coffee to the cream and egg yolk mixture. Freeze the mocha overnight before eating.To Serve: Remove from the loaf tin, cut into 4-6 portions. Serve with raspberry coulis. (Serves 4-6)

The Udny Arms Hotel overlooks the Ythan Estuary, an area noted for its natural beauty and known especially to nature lovers, walkers and sportsmen. On a sunny winter day, nothing is more beautiful than miles of sandy beach and waves crashing on the shore. During winter you may, be lucky enough to have the whole beach to yourself - what a pleasure!

The Udny Arms itself is a handsome Victorian building. The hotel bistro is the most popular area for eating with a view over the Newburgh Golf course. The menu changes on a regular six-weekly basis, and seafood is a speciality. Game bought locally from the well-known dealers, Bain of Tarves is a most popular feature of the menu. In the Parlour, a brasserie style restaurant provides an extensive Table d' hote menu.

My very first experience of Sticky Toffee Pudding was here, as a student nurse, on pay day! We heard it was the best sticky toffee around and were not disappointed. Even though I can afford the cost today better than the calories, it's still a must!

Duck & Fois Gras Paté

Ingredients

600g fois gras
600g duck livers
400g cream
250g butter (melted)
250ml brandy, port or Madeira
14 eggs
Seasoning to taste
2 tablespoons pink salt
2 cloves garlic
1 stem thyme

Method

1. Blend duck livers and fois gras in a food processor.

2. Reduce alcohol in pan with garlic and thyme to half quantity.

3. Mix eggs and cream in a bowl, add pink salt and alcohol.

4. Sieve blended livers into the mixture, mix well, add seasoning and melted butter.

5. Pour mixture into lined terrine.

6. Place in Bain-marie and cook for 3 hours at 170°C/325°F/gas mark 3.

Chef's Tip : Pink salt is a French product which gives the terraine a more attractive colour when cooked, acceptable to both the eye and palate. (Serves 24)

Main Course

Créole Bouillabaisse

Ingredients

2.5kg mixed fish (monkfish, salmon, langoustine, cockles, mussels and plaice fillet)
100mls olive oil
1 onion finely chopped
1 celery stick finely chopped
1 red pepper de-seeded and diced
½ green pepper de-seeded and diced
2 garlic cloves finely chopped
¼ teaspoon dried chilli flakes
Pinch saffron strands
2 tablespoons chopped parsley
Freshly chopped thyme to garnish
1 bay leaf
500g ripe tomatoes, skinned, de-seeded and chopped
1 litre fish stock
Salt and pepper to taste
500g raw prawns or tiger prawns

Method

1. Remove scales and bones from fish and cut into small equal size pieces.

2. Heat the oil in a large casserole and add the onion, celery, peppers, garlic and chilli flakes.

3. Crumble saffron strands and add to the vegetables.

4. Cook gently for 5 minutes, stirring occasionally.

5. Add the herbs, tomatoes, fish stock and seasoning. Stir to mix and bring to the boil.

6. Lower heat and simmer for 30 minutes.

7. Bring back to the boil and add firm-fleshed fish. Cook for 8 minutes stirring gently once or twice.

8. Add pieces of soft-fleshed fish and cook for a further 6 minutes, adding prawns after 2 minutes. Serve with a sprinkling of chopped thyme. (Serves 15)

Dessert

Sticky Toffee Pudding

Ingredients

The Mixture :

¼lb margarine or butter
¾lb caster sugar
2 eggs
1lb self raising flour
1 x 8oz packet dates
1 teaspoon bicarbonate of soda
1 pint boiling water

The Sauce :

½lb butter
1lb brown sugar
1 pint double cream

Method

1.   Cream the butter and sugar until white and fluffy.

2.   Beat in the eggs gradually. Fold in the flour.

3.   In a separate bowl, pour boiling water over the dates and bicarbonate of soda.

4.   When the water has been absorbed, add the dates to the creamed mixture.

5.   Bake in a hot oven for approximately 40 minutes at 160°C / 312°F / gas mark 2 or until firm to the touch.

To make the Sauce

1.   Melt all ingredients together in a heavy-based pan, bring to the boil. Boil for 2 minutes.

2.   Pour over the baked pudding and brown under the grill before serving. (Serves 4-6)

The Silver Darling
Starter

The Silver Darling
Main Course

The Silver Darling
Pudding

The Tolbooth
Starter

The Tolbooth
Main Course

The Tolbooth
Pudding

THE WHITE COTTAGE RESTAURANT

The award-winning White Cottage Restaurant in the heart of Royal Deeside was formerly two estate cottages. Over the last ten years the proprietors Laurie and Josephine Hill have transformed the cottages into a delightful, informal restaurant, renowned throughout the area for the presentation of first class Scottish food. Mr. Hill takes pride in his use of local ingredients and allows the flavours to simply come together on the plate. Vegetarian alternatives are available on the menu.

Meals are often eaten either in the pine-floored dining room, with the open log fire in the winter, or in the conservatory overlooking the garden and pond in the summer months. Their commitment to food and high standards throughout the restaurant, have been well rewarded. They have won The Good Food Guide special award "Restaurant of the Year" and their recommendations include Michelin and Taste of Scotland, and they were awarded two rosettes by the AA.

Starter

Little Pan-Fried Rosti Crab Cakes

Ingredients

4 medium potatoes (King Edwards)
6oz white crab meat- fresh only
Pinch of cayenne pepper
½ teaspoon salt
½ small leek- finely chopped
6oz butter- clarified

Method

1. Grate the raw potatoes and place in the middle of a strong cotton tea towel - wringing excess moisture from the potatoes.

2. Combine the first five ingredients thoroughly until they bind together.

3. Shape into patties (golf ball size) and, when ready to cook, place gently in hot clarified butter in a shallow pan. Flatten slightly, fry both sides, then drain on absorbent paper.

4. Serve with curly endive and Lollo Rosso lettuce with lemon zest or oven dried tomatoes in olive oil, or red onion confit.

Chef's Tip : These cakes must be handled with extreme care otherwise they will break up before they are cooked. (Serves 4)

Main Course

Howtowdie Pheasant Wi' Drappit Eggs

Ingredients

1 hen pheasant
1 cock pheasant
Save the pheasant liver for the gravy

For the Stuffing :
8oz fine white breadcrumbs
1 onion (finely chopped)
Chopped parsley, thyme and marjoram
½tsp paprika
5oz bacon (fried and diced)
1oz melted butter

For the Spinach :
2lb spinach
1oz butter
2fl oz double cream
Grated fresh nutmeg
Seasoning to taste

For the Dish :
4oz clarified butter
2 large onions (sliced)
6 peppercorns
2 cloves
6 standard eggs
3 allspice berries
1pt chicken stock
Salt

Method

1. Prepare birds for cooking, your local butcher would do this for you at very little cost.

2. Prepare the stuffing : Mix the breadcrumbs with the onion, chopped herbs, paprika and bacon. Bind with 1oz of melted butter, cool and stuff the birds with this mixture.

3. For the dish : Heat 4oz clarified butter in a large pan until very hot. Add the birds and brown all over. Remove from the pan and add the onions, sauté for a few minutes until they become opaque. Add the peppercorns, cloves, allspice berries stock and salt, bring to the boil and add the birds back into the pan. Cover and bake in a slow oven 150°C/300°F/gas mark 2 for 1½ hours or until the meat is tender.

4.   For the spinach : Place the spinach in boiling water for 1 minute to wilt the leaves, press out excess water. Puree spinach and beat in the butter, cream and nutmeg.

5.   For the gravy : Strain the stock from the cooked birds, add the liver and cook, then rub the liver through a fine sieve, use to thicken gravy. Pour this over the birds before serving. Poach the eggs in the remaining ¼ pt of stock and serve on the spinach, surrounding the dish of pheasant. (Serves 4)

Warm Prune and Armagnac Pie with Crème Fraîche Ice-Cream

Ingredients

For the Pie :
8oz sweet shortcrust pastry or flaky pastry
8oz French prunes (ready to eat)
1oz cornflour
Egg and milk to glaze
4oz caster sugar
1 wine glass Armagnac

Method

1. Soak the prunes in Armagnac overnight.

2. Roll pastry as thinly as possible for the base and sides and line an 8" metal flan tin.

3. Place the drained prunes onto the pastry. Sprinkle with sugar and cornflour and add a little of the Armagnac. Use the rest of the pastry to cover the prunes. Seal and crimp the edges.

4. Brush with egg yolk and milk beaten together to glaze.

5. Bake in hot oven (approx 200°C/400°F/gas mark 6) until browned. Serve with Ice-Cream.

Crème Fraîche Ice-Cream

Ingredients

8fl oz crème fraîche
5oz caster sugar
4fl oz milk
1 ½fl oz lemon juice
Zest of lemon if desired

Method

1. Mix all ingredients together well and churn in an ice-cream maker. This ice-cream thaws quickly, so time the serving of prune pie accordingly. (Serves 4-6)

For the Chinese food is not just a passion it's an obsession, and good eating is essential to good living. The Chinese have an expression "Chi fan le mei you?" which means, 'have you eaten yet?'. This is a universal greeting just as we would ask "How are you?", it is also a wish for one's health and happiness. Chinese philosophy maintains that there is more to food than mere sustenance: it is a process of cultivating, selecting, cooking and consuming food as a family which is at the heart of Chinese culture.

We are fortunate to have in Aberdeen Yú's restaurant, whose commitment to these strong family traditions have determined the high standards of Chinese cuisine we are privileged to enjoy!

Butterfly Prawns

Ingredients

450g/1lb uncooked prawns in the shells, headless
15ml/1tsp ground szechuan peppercorns
15ml/1tsp light soy sauce
15ml/1tsp Chinese rice wine or dry sherry
10ml/2tsp cornflour
2 eggs, lightly beaten
60-75ml/4-5tablsp breadcrumbs
Vegetable oil for deep frying
2-3 spring onions, to garnish
Lettuce leaves or crispy seaweed to serve

Method

Shell the prawns, leaving the tails intact. Cut each prawn down the back, remove the back vein, rinse and pat dry. Marinade the prawns in soy sauce, Wine/Sherry and ground szechuan peppercorns, for an hour.

Dip each prawn in cornflour, then egg, then breadcrumbs and deep fry until golden. Serve on lettuce leaves or crispy seaweed and garnish with finely chopped spring onion. (Serves 4)

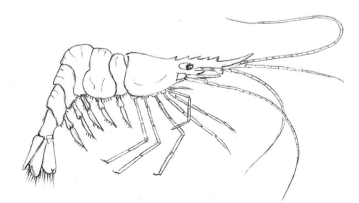

Chicken and Sweetcorn Soup

Ingredients

110g/4oz chicken breast, skinned and finely cubed
10ml/2tsp light soy sauce
15ml/1tablsp Chinese rice wine or dry sherry
5ml/1tsp cornflour
60ml/4tablsp cold water
5ml/1tsp sesame oil
30ml/2tablsp groundnut oil
5ml/1tsp grated fresh root ginger
1 litre/1 ¼ pints/ 4 cups chicken stock
425g/15oz can creamed sweetcorn
225g/8oz can sweetcorn kernels
2 eggs beaten
Salt and ground black pepper
2-3 spring onions, green parts only, cut into tiny rounds to garnish

Method

Sauté the chicken in groundnut oil. In a large saucepan combine the chicken stock, creamed sweetcorn, fresh ginger, sesame oil and bring to the boil. Mix the cornflour to a paste with cold water, add to the soup and stir until the soup boils and thickens. Reduce heat and simmer for one minute.

Beat the eggs with a little extra water, sweet corn kernels, and add to the soup in a steady stream, stirring well. Add the chicken, sweet corn kernels, soy sauce, wine or sherry to the soup and heat gently. Season. Garnish with spring onions. (Serves 4)

Main Course

Fried Shredded Beef

Ingredients

350-400g/12-14oz beef steak
1 large or 2 small carrots
2-3 celery sticks
30ml/2tablsp Chinese rice wine or dry sherry
15ml/1tablsp chilli bean sauce
15ml/1tablsp light soy sauce
1 clove garlic, finely chopped
5ml/1tsp light brown sugar
2-3 spring onions, finely chopped
2.5ml/½tsp finely chopped fresh root ginger
Ground Szechuan peppercorns
Oil

Method

Slice the beef into thin strips. Place the meat in a bowl with the wine/sherry, bean sauce, garlic, ginger and sugar. Marinade for one hour.

Slice the carrots and celery into matchsticks. Heat the oil, brown the meat, add the vegetables and stir-fry. Season with Szechwan pepper and garnish with spring onion. (Serves 4)

A MOTHER'S VIEW

To successfully be the parent of two autistic children for the past twelve years has required patience beyond anything I ever thought I possessed, a skin as thick as a rhinoceros' hide, stamina and a good sense of humour. I have a son of 12 years old and a daughter of 9. Between them we have covered every possible scenario that has ever been described in any literature on autism that I have ever read.

My son was 4 years old before we finally got a diagnosis. He was a very verbal child although his language was never used appropriately and was completely echolalic until he was well over 7 years old. Many people are completely devastated by the diagnosis and grieve for the child that they have lost. After a 2 year fight for his problems to be recognised, I was almost elated that his condition had a name.

My daughter was diagnosed when she was 19 months old. Obviously second time around it was much easier to get people to listen to me. As her problems were very severe, again I found the "autism" label very easy to accept. She was completely non-verbal until she was four years old, very hyperactive and destructive, and she had very severe behavioural problems. I was relieved that, by having a diagnosis, I then had access to information and the Autistic Society and I could then do as much to help my children as possible.

The next few years were a tornado of frustration, total lack of sleep, tantrums, obsessions, eating disorders and just general chaos. My ambition was (and actually still is) to go somewhere quietly as a family without everyone staring at us in total disbelief and without the children's and my own stress levels going through the roof.

Our obsessions included never hanging out washing for over a year. If I tried to sneak anything onto the washing line it was ripped off and a massive tantrum followed. Washing jackets and bedding produced hysteria beyond belief and resulted in my having to wash and dry these things while they slept. Every item in the house had a place and if it were moved an inch chaos ensued. Every single thing we did had a long and complicated ritual associated with it. Sometimes it took an hour to get a drink of juice. The rituals and obsessions are too numerous to mention but it did mean that life was very difficult and every single thing we did had to be planned with military precision.

As the children's understanding improved, this way of life changed. They were and still are obsessive and ritualistic but I am far more able to deal with it and can be amused by it. My son was obsessed with road maps and signs for a while. When asked where he went for a school trip the answer was, "Two give ways, bend to the right, stop and staggered junction". When the teacher checked he was absolutely spot on. Road signs were replaced by dinosaurs, dinosaurs were replaced by The Guinness Book of Records etc etc. Nowadays his whole life revolves around the Sony Playstation and Father Ted. He can still be echolalic and Father Ted has produced some very unsavoury outbursts but I have learned to laugh them off.

My daughter's current obsession is art galleries, of which I have absolutely no knowledge. We traipse around Aberdeen Art Gallery studying each picture in great depth and I am subjected to an endless stream of questions. Does Stonehaven, Peterhead, Spain have art galleries? How many pictures do they have, how big are they, what are they called? It goes on endlessly. She is also devoting a lot of her time to chopping pieces of thread- as they do in the latest Disney film Hercules. Still we have progressed a lot from the sad little girl who didn't even know her own name and who ran around the house jumping from the top of the cooker onto the window sill and ripping up pieces of paper into identical straight lines.

I have a lovely memory of my daughter leaping into a bunker on the golf course, throwing sand in the air and shouting Beach Beach at the top of her voice. To the very cross golfer I apologise and hope he and his family never go through what my family have. Autistic children are usually very big, strong and good looking and I guess it is difficult for members of the public to understand that they can have such a devastating condition when they look 'alright'. However it is hard enough to be the parent of an autistic child without constant criticism.

Autistic children have to be taught every new skill they learn - they very rarely learn anything incidentally. I spent hours and hours working my children's legs and arms to make them build the bricks, stack the toy, climb the chute and very often received a kick or a slap for my trouble. However, I feel in the long run it has paid enormous dividends. My philosophy was to teach them as much about life as I possibly could while they were still young enough to be handled. An autistic child will always opt out of a new and frightening experience and it is far simpler to try a variety of things with a young child who can still be carried rather than wait until they are 12 years old, 5ft6in and 11 stone. I could persuade my son to do anything now even if he didn't want to, and I feel having let him try a wide range of experiences when he was young has helped him decide what he likes doing and he is now more eager to try new things.

As I said previously, some people are devastated at learning that their child is autistic, and have a lot of problems coming to terms with their child's disability.

I had no problem with that but I do feel that for parents with any child who has special needs, it is a continual grieving process. Most of the time you cope on a day-to-day basis but certain things can trigger off sadness and remind you that life is different. When I see younger children out playing in the street or the park, it reminds me that my two are at home under constant supervision. When my son can't do his homework sheet on best friends because he hasn't got one, that is hard for me as a parent to deal with.

One of our constant sources of comfort, information, friendship and independence for both the children and myself has been through the local Autistic Society at the Jigsaw Centre. My children go to the playschemes on a regular basis which gives me a break, but more importantly gives them a chance to enjoy themselves without me, in an environment completely suited to their needs. It has given them the opportunity to meet other young people with similar problems and from that friendships are beginning to evolve. For myself and my husband it is a chance to meet other families with similar difficulties and to share experiences.

Although the last twelve years have been difficult and we have faced many problems, I would never change my children who are my inspiration. They have overcome many difficulties and try so hard to get on with life which can be very stressful for them at times. Perhaps we are not the average family but we have a lot of fun and appreciate the things they have learned to do. Life is always interesting and I am never sure what they will do or say next. I cringe every time we meet a person who is perhaps overweight, or has a spot or a large nose because at least one, or both of them, will point it out in a very loud voice without the slightest knowledge that they may cause offence or hurt someone's feelings.

Having an autistic child in the family is devastating, not only for the child itself, the parents and siblings but also for the grandparents, aunts, uncles, cousins and anyone whose lives are touched by the child. The way forward is for more centres like Jigsaw, information and support for all members of the family, more public awareness and infinite support for the youngsters. By buying this book you are helping my children and many others to enjoy their lives as well as you enjoying all the wonderful recipes. Please remember them every time you use it!

Scottish Society for Autistic Children (SAAC)

The SAAC is the biggest provider of services for Autism in Scotland. It provides specialist care, support and education to help people with Autism, and their families make the most of their lives. They operate a residential school for children, training and supported living for young adults, respite care and community support services, training for carers and professionals, and giving advice and information. They are especially dependant on the generosity of others to fulfil demands for family support services, information and development of respite care.

Additionally, the Society offers advisory and information services for parents and professionals, supports local parents groups and societies, organises workgroups and produces an information pack, a members magazine and newsletter. Advice on all aspects of Autism is available from our professional staff.

For further information on Autism or the SAAC please contact:

Maria Rybak or Helen Petrie, Appeals and Marketing Department SAAC Headquarters.

SSACC Headquarters
Hilton House
Alloa Business Park
Whins Road
Alloa
FK10 35A

Tel: (01259) 720044
Fax: (01259) 720051
E-mail: ssacc@autism-in-scotland.org.uk

ACKNOWLEDGEMENTS

Donations were gratefully recieved to support the book, from which all proceeds will go to The Grampian Autistic Society.

Aboyne Fund Raise
Amerada Hess
Amoco (UK) Exploration
Bain of Tarves
BP Exploration (Scotland)
Briscot Limited
Chevron (UK) Limited
Chris and Nigel Wooley
Connors Seafood
Conoco (UK)Ltd
Diane Lloyd
Dorling Kindersley
DSND Oceantech Limited
Ellon Inner Wheel
Ellon Lions Club
Ellon Raft Race
Ellon Rotary Club
Ellon Round Table
Fircroft Group
Gilcomston Litho (Aberdeen) Limited
Grampian Country Food group
Kvaerner Oil
Macphie Ingredients
Marathon Oil
Mick & Helen Longton
Oil Industry Community Fund
Peterhead Inner Wheel
RDS Resource Limited
Royal Bank of Scotland
Scofish International Limited
Shell UK Exploration & Production
Stena Offshore
Subsea Offshore Limited
Topstory
Turriff Rotary Club
Udny Green Dancing Class
Wiggins Teape for donation of paper

Hotels and Restaurants

Ardoe House Hotel
South Deeside Road
Aberdeen
AB12 5YP

Cameron House Hotel
Loch Lomond, Alexandria
Dunbartonshire
G83 8QZ

Casa Salvatore
41 Station Road
Ellon
AB41 9AR

The Cock & Bull Brasserie
Ellon Road
Balmedie
AB23 8BX

The Courtyard
1 Alford Lane
Aberdeen
AB1 1YD

Craigellachie Hotel
Victoria Street
Craigellachie
AB38 9SR

Nairns
13 Woodside Crescant
Glasgow
G3 7UP

Nosheen Tandoori Restaurant
Bridge Street
Ellon
AB41 9AA

The Green Inn Restaurant
9 Victoria Road
Ballater
AB35 5QQ

The Lairhillock
Netherley, By Stonehaven
Aberdeenshire
AB39 3QS

Les Amis
58-60 Justice Mill Lane
Aberdeen
AB11 6EP

The Marcliffe Hotel at Pitfodels
North Deeside Road
Aberdeen
AB15 9YA

Meldrum House Hotel
Oldmeldrum
Aberdeenshire
AB51 0AE

Lady McDonald
Kinloch Lodge
Sleat, Isle of Skye
IV43 8QY

Faraday's
2 Kirk Brae, Cults
Aberdeen
AB15 9SQ

Farleyer House Hotel
Aberfeldy
Perthshire
PH15 2JE

Gleneagles Hotel
Auchterarder
Perthshire
PH3 1NF

The Royal Thai
29 Crown Terrace
Aberdeen
AB11 6HD

Simpson's Hotel, Bar & Brasserie
59-63 Queens Road
Aberdeen
AB15 4YE

The Tolbooth
Old Pier
Stonehaven
AB3 2JU

The White Cottage
Dess, Aboyne
Aberdeenshire
AB34 5BP

Pittodrie House Hotel
Chapel of Garioch
By Inverurie
AB51 5HS

Q Brasserie
9 Alford Place
Aberdeen
AB10 1YD

The Silver Darling
Porca Quay, North Pier
Aberdeen
AB11 5DQ

Thainstone House Hotel
Inverurie
Aberdeenshire
AB51 5NT

The Udny Arms Hotel
Main Street
Newburgh
AB41 6BL

Yú
347 Union Street
Aberdeen
AB11 6BT

GLOSSARY OF TERMS

Aïoli is a type of Provençal mayonnaise sauce.

al dente is an Italian expression meaning 'to the tooth', the phrase denotes the proper texture of the pasta or risotto rice.

Aramatic salt to be found in Indian grocers.

Aubergine (egg plant) is a vegetable whose original home is Asia, but is probably associated more with Mediterranean countries.

Bain-marie is a large, water filled pan in which smaller dishes are set for cooking when indirect gentle heat is required.

Balsamic Vinegar has been made in Modena in Italy for centuries. Fresh grape juice is boiled for a day then transferred to wooden vats for ageing.

Bhindi is a vegetable used widely in Indian cookery, they are known as 'ladies fingers or Okra'.

Blanch plunge food into boiling water

Brunoise is a term applied to the method of cutting vegetables into very small dice.

Butternut Squash is a vegetable.

Cassia Bark is a highly aromatic tree bark used all over Asia in cookery. Cassia and cinnamon may be used interchangeably.

Chantilly Cream is fresh cream beaten to the consistency of a mousse.

Chanterelles are a type of mushroom mushroom which can be bought at any good supermarket.

Chiffonade involves cutting into strips of varying thickness.

Chinois is a conical strainer with a handle.

Clarify involves melting and straining butter of it's milk particles; to clear jellies and stocks by filtering.

Concassée is a French term used for chopping or pounding a substance either coarsely or finely.

Confit is a piece of pork, goose, duck or turkey cooked in its own fat and stored in a pot, covered in the same fat to preserve it.

Consommé is a meat, poultry or fish stock served hot or cold, generally at dinner.

Coulis is a liquid puree.

Croustade are small cases made of bread, brushed with butter and baked or deep fried until crisp.

Dariole are small steep sided cylindrical moulds used in the preparation of pastries, rice puddings or vegetable pasties.

Deglaze is to heat wine, stock or other liquid together with the cooking juices and sediment left in the pan, after roasting or sautéing in order to make a sauce or gravy.

Duchesse-Purée of potatoes, blended with eggs and butter, puped into a border and baked.

Feuilles de brie is Moroccan filo pastry

Fish Sauce is an essential cooking ingredient in South East Asian countries. It is made from a liquid of dried fermented anchovies.

Fondant is a sugar syrup containing glucose, cooked to the 'soft ball' stage then worked with a spatula until it becomes a thick opaque paste. This can be bought from any good confectioner.

Ganache is a flavoured cream made with chocolate, butter and fresh cream used to decorate desserts.

Gelatine Leaves are used by professionals in the same way as powder for making jellies and numerous cold desserts.

Ghee is a butter used in Indian cookery that has been so well clarified, that you can use it, to deep fry.

Juniper Berries are a shrub best known for the distinctive flavour it gives to gin.

Jus-Lie Stock

Karahi is an Indian cooking utensil, similar to the Chinese wok.

Karela a bitter gourd.

Kumquats are very small fruit of the orange variety, originating in China. They can be bought from any good supermarket.

Lemon Grass is a tough fleshy grass with sharp edges, used for its intense flavour in South East Asian food.

Langoustines originate from the shellfish family.

Maldon Salt is not as coarse as sea salt and better by far than regular salt.

Mascarpone Cheese is a fresh thick cream cheese originally from Lombardy and Piedmont. It is made with cow's milk.

Mousseline is any mousse-like preparation and which would usually have a quantity of whipped cream added to it.

Nage is a marinated vegetable stock.

Pancetta is a streaky bacon coming from the belly of a pig.

Panden Leaves are used for their distinctive flavour. They are sometimes green and are often used for Thai cookery.

Parfait is an iced dessert made with fresh cream which gives it smoothness and prevents it from melting too quickly.

Pink Salt is used to give terrines a pink colour once cooked, to make them more palatable looking.

Praline is a delicate filling for sweets and chocolates, consisting of lightly roasted almonds or hazelnuts mixed with sugar then crushed in cocoa.

Puy Lentils are small lentils coloured from green to brown to blue, now grown in Italy as well as in France.

Quenelles are a light fish or meat dumpling usually poached.

Ramekins are small individual oven dishes usually made of porcelain.

Refresh is to rinse freshly cooked food in cold water to halt the cooking process and set the colour.

Ribbon Stage is reached in the beating of a mixture when a ribbon trail is left as the beaters are lifted.

Sabayon is a frothy, sweet sauce of whipped egg yolks, sugar, wine and liqueur.

Sablé is a crumbly biscuit of varying size, made from flour, butter and egg yolks.

Salsa is a spicy Mexican condiment.

Sauté is to cook meat, fish or vegetables in fat until brown.

Shiitake Mushrooms are mushrooms used in Chinese cookery.

Tamarind is a fibrous pod used in curries and soups for its acidic effect, mostly in Thai cookery.

Terrine is a pate or minced mixture cooked in a loaf shaped mould.

Timbale is a dish cooked in a drum shaped mould.

Tinda is a squash.

Zhoug Relish is a relish originally from the Yemen.

Description	Degrees Celsius	Degrees Fahrenheit	Gas Mark
Very Cool	110	225	1/4
	120	250	1/2
Cool	140	275	1
	150	300	2
Moderate	160	325	3
	180	350	4
Moderately Hot	190	375	5
	200	400	6
Hot	220	425	7
	230	450	8
Very Hot	240	475	9

Hidden Kitchens of the North

Index

Q

Quails
Roasted with Wild Mushrooms 34

R

Raspberry
Cake 76
Cratins 93

Red Cabbage 84

Rhubarb
& Toffee Crumble 114

Risolto .138

S

Sabayon
Pear & Chocolate 143

Salad
Bacon 70
Chargrilled Salmon 99

Salmon
& Scallop 83
Ballotine of 21
Mousse 169
Pan Fried 55
Salad 99
Smoked ~ Crepes 95
Smoked with Scallops & Langoustines 100

Salsa
Tomato 89

Sauce
Butterscotch 27

Scallops
& Crab Mousseline 32
& Salmon 83
Seared with Chervil Butter 140
with Smoked Salmon & Languistines 100

Seafood
Butterfly Prawns 188
Chuni Prawns 147
Crab Cakes 182
King Prawn Bhoona 128
Mixed with Sweet Pepper Risotto . . . 100
Mosaic of with Vegetables 108
Potted Scallop & Salmon 83
Rosette of Seared Scallops 140
Scallop & Crab Mousseline 32
Thai 146

Shortbread
Tartlet 61

Soufflé
Glayva & Honey 72
Haddock 45
Lemon & Vanilla 97

Soup
Chicken & Sweetcorn 189
Curried Banana 74
Rabbit & Aubergone 20
Roasted Red Pepper 166
Wild Mushroom 116

Steak
with Bananas & Chestnuts 75

Sticky Toffee Pudding 27

Strawberries
Deep Fried 30

Sugar Springs 87

T

V

W